Confession and Absolution

BEING THE SIXTH BOOK OF THE LAWS
OF ECCLESIASTICAL POLITY BY THAT
LEARNED AND JUDICIOUS DIVINE
MR. RICHARD HOOKER

EDITED (WITH INTRODUCTION, ANALYSIS,
NOTES, AND APPENDIX) BY THE
REV. JOHN HARDING M.A
VICAR OF COLDHARBOUR, SURREY:
AND
LATE SCHOLAR OF BRASENOSE COLLEGE, OXFORD

LONDON:
CHARLES MURRAY 11 LUDGATE SQUARE E.C
1901

In the interest of creating a more extensive selection of rare historical book reprints, we have chosen to reproduce this title even though it may possibly have occasional imperfections such as missing and blurred pages, missing text, poor pictures, markings, dark backgrounds and other reproduction issues beyond our control. Because this work is culturally important, we have made it available as a part of our commitment to protecting, preserving and promoting the world's literature. Thank you for your understanding.

ABSOLUTION

INTRODUCTION.

AT a time when the subjects of Confession and Absolution occupy such a prominent place in the religious controversies of the day, it may be useful to place before our minds the well-considered views of one whose name has been honoured in the Church of England for more than three centuries. It is, perhaps, one of the faults of a more hurrying age, that religious doctrines and practices are often handled in a loose and superficial manner, and without sufficient knowledge of the facts of history. These, when properly weighed, are found exceedingly valuable, and help us in arriving at just conclusions thereon.

Let me endeavour, by way of introduction, to set before the reader a brief sketch of the life of Richard Hooker, and of the character of the times in which he lived.

It appears, from the interesting and admirable memoir prefixed to the Oxford edition of his works, and written by the famous Izaak Walton, that Richard Hooker was born in or near the city of Exeter, about the year 1553; that he was educated, first in his native city, and afterwards, by the good offices and assistance of Bishop Jewel, of Salisbury, at Corpus Christi College, Oxford; and that both at school and at college he showed himself not only apt and diligent, and of quick apprehension in all kinds of knowledge, but also devout and earnest in his religion, and ever increasing, not only in learning, but in piety.

Admitted as Fellow of Corpus in 1577, Richard Hooker remained and studied there until the time of his ordination in (or about) 1581. In the same year he seems to have been summoned (probably by the Bishop of London) to preach at St. Paul's Cross in London. For the incidents attaching to this journey, and the unhappy marriage to which it ultimately led, we must be content to refer our readers to the inimitably quaint account of the same in the pages of Izaak Walton. Suffice it to say that in 1584 we find Hooker settled in his country living of Drayton Beauchamp; married to one who "brought him neither beauty nor portion"; but still intent upon his sacred duties and studies, and ready (as he himself put it to his favourite pupils, who had come to see their former tutor) "not to repine at what my wise Creator hath appointed for me, but . . . to submit mine to His will, and possess my soul in patience and peace."

We constantly observe that the current of men's lives seems directed by apparently trivial circumstances; rather we should say, that a wise Providence orders and arranges their minutest details. This visit of Hooker's pupils (one of whom was Edwin Sandys, son of the Archbishop of York, and the other George Cranmer, grand-nephew of Archbishop Cranmer) was the indirect cause of his advancement to the position of Master of the Temple. For Edwin Sandys, begging of his father for some more quiet and comfortable position for his former preceptor, and the position above mentioned falling vacant, Richard Hooker was, in 1585, appointed, through the influence of Archbishop Sandys, to that office, for which his piety and learning rendered him eminently fit.

The six years between 1585 and 1591, during which he occupied this distinguished position, were not years of peace and quietness with our author; for we find him constantly engaged in controversy with Mr. Walter Travers, who, indeed, during some portion of the time, was afternoon lecturer at the Temple. The differences of views between these two were of a pronounced character; insomuch that, to use the quaint language of Fuller (*Worthies of England*, p. 264), "the pulpit spake pure Canterbury in the morning, and Geneva in the afternoon, until Travers was silenced." At length, the Archbishop of Canterbury (Whitgift) deeming it wise to prohibit Travers from preaching, the controversy between the two divines became of a more public character, Travers attacking his opponent's views with no little earnestness, and Hooker justifying them with learning and patience. We may trace, indeed, in this controversy, the origin of the *Ecclesiastical Polity* itself; as to which it may be well to quote the very words of Izaak Walton.

"After the publication of his *Answer to the Petition of Mr. Travers*, Mr. Hooker grew daily into greater repute with the most learned and wise of the nation; but it had a contrary effect in very many of the Temple that were zealous for Mr. Travers and for his Church discipline; insomuch that, though Mr. Travers left the place, yet the seeds of discontent could not be rooted out of that society, by the great reason, and as great meekness, of this humble man; for though the chief benchers gave him much reverence and encouragement, yet he there met with many neglects and oppositions by those of Master Travers' judgment; insomuch that it turned to his extreme grief; and that he might unbeguile and win them, he designed to write a deliberate sober Treatise of the Church's power to make canons for the use of ceremonies, and by law to impose an obedience to them, as upon her children: and this he proposed to do in eight books of the *Laws of Ecclesiastical Polity*; intending therein to shew such arguments as should force an assent from all men, if reason delivered in sweet language, and void of any provocation, were able to do it."

To give himself more leisure for the prosecution of this his design, Richard Hooker craved of the Archbishop of Canterbury some quiet country living, saying that "God and nature had not intended him for contentions, but for study and quietness." He was thereupon, by the Archbishop, appointed to the living of Boscum, near Salisbury, at which place four books of the *Polity* were prepared. These were published in 1594.

In 1595 he was appointed to the parish of Bishopsbourne, near Canterbury, where, by a holy and studious life, he once again commended himself to the parishioners and neighbours. He is described by an eye-witness as an "obscure, harmless man: a man in poor clothes, his loins usually girt in a coarse gown, or canonical coat: of a mean stature, and stooping, and yet more lowly in the thoughts of his soul: his body worn out, not with age, but study and holy mortifications." Neither yet did this good man escape from malicious accusations as to his moral character and conduct—which, being as patiently borne as they were falsely invented, were at length, by the good offices and diligence of his devoted friends, Edwin Sandys and George Cranmer, absolutely disproved, so that his accusers were themselves forced to confess his innocence.

There is abundant evidence that before his death at Bishopsbourne, in 1600, the whole of the eight books of the *Ecclesiastical Polity* were completed. The first four of these were published in 1594; the fifth by itself, in 1597. The remaining three books seem to have been published, not from Hooker's completed MSS., but from the rough draught of them, which came into the hands of Archbishop Whitgift, and was by him committed to the editorship of Dr. Spenser, a lifelong friend of Hooker, and afterwards President of Corpus. Dr. Spenser, in his preface to the first five books, published together in 1604, states that "there is a purpose of setting forth the three last books also, their father's *Posthumi*. For as in the great declining of his body, spent out with study, it was his ordinary petition to Almighty God that, if he might live to see the finishing of these books, then, *Lord, let thy servant depart in peace,* (to use his own words,) so it pleased God to grant him his desire. For he lived till he saw them perfected. . . . But some evil-disposed minds, whether of malice, or covetousness, or wicked blind zeal, it is uncertain, as if they had been Egyptian midwives, as soon as they were born, and their father dead, smothered them, and by conveying away the perfect copies, left unto us nothing but certain old, imperfect and mangled draughts, dismembered into pieces, . . . not the shadows of themselves almost remaining in them. . . . But seeing the importunities of many great and worthy persons will not suffer them quietly to die and to be buried, it is intended that they shall see them as they are. The learned and judicious eye will yet perhaps delight itself in beholding the goodly lineaments of their well set bodies, and in finding out some shadows and resemblances of their father's face."

Dr. Spenser's intention to publish the three remaining books was, however, not carried out by himself. Much of the necessary work was done under his direction; but at his death, in 1614, the whole of Hooker's papers seem to have passed to Dr. King, Bishop of London; then to Lambeth Library, where they were under the charge successively of Archbishops Abbot, Laud, and Ussher. In the year 1651 there came out, *Of the Laws of Ecclesiasticall Policy, the Sixth and Eighth Books. By Richard Hooker. A work long expected, and now published, according to the most authentique copies.* The seventh book appears not to have seen the light until 1662, when it was published by Gauden, Bishop of Worcester.

The Sixth Book of the *Polity*—as it stands in the collected edition, and as now published in separate form —appears to treat of quite a different subject from that which is appointed for it in the sketch of the whole work, or " What Things are handled in the Books following," which is prefixed to the collected edition. The subject assigned to Book VI. is, "Of the Power of Jurisdiction, which the reformed platform claimeth unto lay-elders, with others."

It will at once be noted that the actual subject of the book, as we have it at present, is the doctrine concerning Confession and Absolution. What confirms the idea that the original Sixth Book has been replaced by the well-reasoned treatise contained in this little volume, is the existence of a MS. in the library of Corpus Christi College, Oxford, containing the original notes and comments of Hooker's two favourite pupils (in the handwriting of each) upon the original Sixth Book. It is evident from these notes and comments that our author had adhered to his original design, and discussed the subject of Lay-Government in the Church; it being even possible to reconstruct his line of argument from the remarks made thereon by his pupils. We need not, however, regret that those who were responsible for putting forth the *Ecclesiastical Polity* saw fit to include in it this treatise upon Confession. There can be little doubt that the original Sixth Book upon Lay-Government in the Church would have been the first to perish, if it fell (as appears above) into the hands of his Puritan adversaries. But we of these days may be thankful that such a wise, sober, and judicious treatise upon the subject which it discusses (a treatise, it may be added incidentally, which has passed under the critical and discriminating eye of Archbishop Ussher, the fruit of whose ripe judgment appears in the present text of the work) should have been preserved for the instruction of the generations to come. May we not even say that the hand of a good Providence can herein be seen, overruling all events, and causing the "wrath of man" to "turn to His praise"?

It remains for me to add a few words, as to the times in which Richard Hooker lived, and the general character of the religious world in his day.

When, in the year 1558, Queen Mary died, and her sister Elizabeth succeeded to the throne of England, it was natural that the Reformers, many of whom were in exile upon the Continent, should return as speedily as possible to the country from which persecutions had banished them. But in many cases, their proceedings were extremely ill-advised. Thinking that the tide had turned in their own favour, they began "to deface images, demolish altars, and to preach, both privately and openly, the extreme reforming views which they had learned abroad." But the Queen, though she had already shown signs of willingness to favour the reform of the Church, was not prepared to countenance these proceedings, as they had expected. She had to deal with matters with a view to political considerations, as well as to those of religion. Her first work was to appoint a commission for the revision of Edward VI's. second Prayer Book, and, meanwhile, to issue a proclamation, commanding moderation in religious teaching, and to enforce, through her own Lord Keeper (at the opening of Parliament 1559), the duties of reverent worship on the one hand, and the giving over of idolatrous or superstitious practices on the other.[1] Formal disputations between selected champions on the Romanist and the Reforming sides were held in Westminster Abbey. The bishops not accepting the Act of Supremacy were (with one exception) deprived of their sees. New prelates (and at this point comes in the incident of the Nag's Head fable) had to be appointed and consecrated. Amongst these we find the names of Sandys, Bishop of Worcester (afterwards Archbishop of York, and father to Richard Hooker's pupil), and Jewel, Bishop of Salisbury, his friend and patron, as mentioned above.

Those who were responsible for the affairs of the Church in those days, had indeed an anxious and a difficult position. The condition of the country clergy was lamentable. Many parishes were without clergy. "There is a great and alarming scarcity of preachers," says Bishop Jewel; "our schools and universities are deserted."

Upon the whole, it may be said that the bishops and Convocation acted in a wise and prudent manner. The Articles (then only Thirty-Eight in number) were agreed upon by Convocation in 1562 (O.S.), and sanctioned by the Queen in the following year. In the same year (1563) appeared Bishop Jewel's famous *Apology of the Church of England.* But it will be, perhaps, hardly wrong to say (indeed, it was only what might be expected) that the preponderance of opinion amongst the bishops was in favour of the Reformation rather than the Romanist views; and the chief

---

[1] D'Ewes : Journals of Queen Elizabeth's Parliaments, p. 12.

difficulty experienced by Archbishop Parker was with those inclining to Calvinistic doctrines and views. He was himself a man of firmness, though moderate in his own views, and has been well described as "a fair-judging, temperate, earnest man at a time of great anxiety and difficulty. He was also especially valuable to the Church as an organizer at a time of change and confusion."

Archbishop Parker was succeeded by Archbishop Grindal, himself inclined by disposition to Puritan views. We need not perhaps linger upon the eight years of his primacy, except to observe that (as was natural) the Puritan party felt themselves encouraged to proceed more openly. He was succeeded in 1583 by Archbishop Whitgift, who found the difficulties of the Church by no means diminished, but rather increased, by the conduct of his predecessor.

We have now nearly arrived at the year (1585) when Richard Hooker was made Master of the Temple. It will easily be seen that the times were those which rendered the presence in such a responsible position of one whose learning and piety were both above suspicion —a most important accession to the strength of the Church of England. Both the universities were strongly Puritan. Dr. John Reynolds, the President of Corpus in Hooker's time, was a staunch champion of Puritan views. It is Heylin who tells us that "the face of the university was so much altered, that there was little to be seen in it of the Church of England according to the principles and positions upon which it was first reformed."[1] At Cambridge "there were, through the reign of Elizabeth, many more distinguished men than at Oxford, but the Puritanism and Calvinism of Cambridge had been even more decided and aggressive." From Trinity College came Cartwright and Travers, the "head and neck" of English Puritanism, while "Drs. Humphrey and Reynolds of Oxford were eclipsed in their Calvinism by Drs. Whitaker and Good at Cambridge."

---

[1] Heylin's Life of Laud, p. 57.

We shall probably be ready to agree with the view expressed by the Rev. John Keble in his preface to the Oxford edition of Hooker's works, that "in the annals of the Church, with more certainty perhaps than in those of the world, we may from time to time mark out what may be called *turning points*: points in which every thing seems to depend upon some one critical event or coincidence at the time, possibly, quite unobserved. . . . One of these critical periods in our own Church history, if the editor mistake not, is the latter portion of the sixteenth century; and the character and views of Hooker mark him (if we may venture to judge of such a thing without irreverence) as one specially raised up to be the chief human instrument in the salutary interference which Divine Providence was then preparing."

One point should, in conclusion, be noted, prior to the careful study which the treatise upon Confession and Absolution deserves. It is this: that the first and natural leanings of our author were rather in the Puritan direction than any other; and that therefore, in the examination of the questions involved, he was not likely to be biassed by any undue inclination towards the errors of Rome. On the other hand, we may observe that the times in which he lived were such as to render every true son of the Church as careful to maintain reverence, and to uphold the Church's order, as to resist error and superstition. So that we are not surprised to see our author holding a just and true balance between Romish pretensions on the one hand, and irreverent neglect on the other; and in this, as well as other matters, deserving that epithet of "judicious," which succeeding ages have bestowed upon him.

With these observations—all of which have been designed to make both the personality of Richard Hooker, and the character of the times in which he lived, more real and vivid to the mind of the reader than they would otherwise have been—I commend this Sixth Book of the *Polity* to his earnest consideration, praying that the blessing of God may rest upon its publication in separate form. I have added, by way of Appendix, short notices of most of the writers, especially the Fathers of the Church, to whom our author makes reference in this treatise. A perusal of these will make clearer to our minds the wide range of Hooker's studies, and his complete mastery of the subject on which he writes.

J. H.

COLDHARBOUR VICARAGE, SURREY,
7th October, 1900.

NOTE.

THE text which I have followed is, in the main, that of the Oxford edition of Hooker's Works, published in 1839. It has been slightly altered, in one or two places, by a comparison of the latest edition of the same, revised by Dean Church and Dr. Paget, from which edition the division into sections has also been adopted. Notes taken from the last-named edition are acknowledged by the letters ("C. and P.").

Analysis of the Contents of this Book.

CHAPTER I.

OUGHT LAY ELDERS TO HAVE AUTHORITY IN SPIRITUAL CAUSES?

Sect. I.—The question between us (*i.e.* Churchmen and Puritans) is, whether all congregations or parishes ought to have lay-elders invested with power of jurisdiction in spiritual causes.

Sect. II.—The Puritan leaders are of opinion that their whole scheme of public service, etc., requires the support of the laity for its introduction; and that this will be the more readily given if such authority be placed in their hands.

Sect. III.—The twofold advantage of such a course: the people favour it, as being for their own interest; and the pretended divine authority gives encouragement for hope of good success in their enterprises.

Sect. IV.—It is well, however, that such as uphold this view, should consider whether the history of Korah and his company (Num. xvi. 3) be not applicable to their own circumstances.

CHAPTER II.

THE NATURE OF SPIRITUAL JURISDICTION.

Sect. I.—The difference that exists between the power of ecclesiastical *jurisdiction* and that of ecclesiastical *order*.

Sect. II.—The first of these comes to the Church as a gift from Christ Himself; the other is (under Divine guidance) arranged by the Church, according to the variety of times, circumstances, etc., in which she is placed.

[At this point we notice the transition from the original Sixth Book to the treatise upon Confession, Satisfaction, and Absolution, which has now taken its place.]

CHAPTER III.

OF PENITENCE.

Sect. I.—There are two kinds of penitence. One is 'a private duty towards God; the other a duty of external discipline. We may distinguish between inward and outward repentance by calling the first the *virtue*, the latter the *discipline*, of repentance. The one is shown towards God, the other towards men; the one is always, the other only in some cases, necessary.

Sect. II.—The *virtue* of repentance is from God only. It is constantly offered to man (Rev. iii. 20). And it is well to note the methods by which the Holy Ghost works to this end. Always, by illuminating the eye of faith; usually, by making the sinner *fear* the judgment of God upon sin. (So St. Peter's sermon on the day of Pentecost; Jonah at Nineveh; our Lord's words concerning Chorazin and Bethsaida; the burning of books at Ephesus, etc. Acts ii. 37; Jonah iii. 5; Matt. xi. 21; Acts xix. 17, 19.)

Sect. III.—But *fear*, in itself, does not produce repentance. We have also to believe (i.) the possibility, and (ii.) the means, of averting evil. Love must be added to fear, before Repentance ensues: the "goodness of God" must move us to repent. God is seen, by the testimony of Holy Scripture, to be full of compassion, and ready to pardon upon man's repentance. "Sweet sentences" from the "grave writings" of the Fathers, *e.g.* Cassian and Basil, confirming this view.

Sect. IV.—The above, illustrated from Holy Scripture itself. David's confession effectual, because fear and love were therein blended; Saul's ineffectual, because only the fear of punishment moved him. The Ninevites first feared, but afterwards had fear tempered by hope (Jonah iii. 9). The prodigal son knew both his own sin and his father's love. We may say, therefore, that "The well-spring of repentance is faith, first breeding fear, and then love."

Sect. V.—The duty of a penitent. Three chief points to be noted: Contrition, Confession, and Satisfaction. Of these three, the first must be deliberate, and does not consist merely in external signs of grief, such as tears, etc., but in the aversion of the will from sin ; and a just sorrow, neither feigned nor slight, for the sin which we have committed.

Sect. VI.—The second and third of the duties named above, viz. Confession and Satisfaction, belong as well to the discipline as to the virtue of repentance. (See above, section i.) The only difference is, that in the one case they are performed to God only, in the other case to men as well. The subjects of Confession and Satisfaction may therefore be handled together, distinguishing only their exercise towards God, and towards men.

CHAPTER IV.

OF REPENTANCE, AND OF CONFESSION.

Sect. I.—The discipline of repentance must be carried out in accordance with that rule and authority which our Lord has given to His Church—in the first place to His Apostles. This rule and authority is a sacred trust. They that have the "keys" are God's stewards: not to profit themselves, but to benefit men's souls. Their duties have to do, not only with doctrine, but with discipline ; and for this latter they have their own appointed courts, in which, whatever is done by way of orderly and lawful proceeding, the Lord Himself has promised to ratify. This is the original warrant, given by our Lord (Matt. xviii. 18 ; John xx. 23), and acted upon by His Apostles (1 Cor. v. 3 ; 2 Cor. ii. 6) and others (1 Tim. i. 20) ; only, however, as was seen to be good and expedient for the cure of sin.

Sect. II.—In former ages, public confession was made by open transgressors in the hearing of the whole Church, and open acts of penitence were appointed. Secret offenders, however, were wont to have their acts of penitence more privately appointed, their public confession following these.

Sect. III.—As time went on, and Christianity became less simple and less loving, it seemed desirable that voluntary penitents should not make open, but private, confession. The Lateran Council (A.D. 1215) decreed that all men should, once a year, confess to the priest. The next step was, that the Church of Rome lifted penitence into a "sacrament of remission of sins after baptism." The illogical results of this theory. Views of Duns Scotus and Thomas Aquinas. The decree of the Council of Trent, approving the doctrine, and ascribing to the *words of absolution* the chief force and operation of their sacrament. It is to be observed that, in

B

18   *Contents*

>   this view, the idea of Satisfaction for injuries done to others forms no part of the so-called sacrament, since it is not performed until after the administration of the sacrament.

Sect. IV.—But is the Romish doctrine concerning compulsory confession a true one? Confession of sin to God is, no doubt, both necessary and desirable. Views of Tertullian and Chrysostom, as to this. Jewish practices concerning confession : (1) the general confession of sins on the Day of Atonement ; (2) voluntary confessions ; (3) special confessions, accompanied by special sacrifices ; (4) confessions invited (*e.g.* Achan) after particular offences. The Jewish Rabbis commended those who were willing to acknowledge their sins before many.

Sect. V.—These confessions, however, were all voluntary. Where, in Holy Scripture, is to be found a commandment for compulsory, to say nothing of auricular, confession ? The confessions made to John the Baptist (Matt. iii. 6), as well as those made at Ephesus (Acts xix. 18), were certainly voluntary. St. James's words (James v. 14, 16) relate to mutual acknowledgment of sins among Christians, and to the exercise by the elders of the Church of the miraculous gifts committed to the early Church, and continued long after the Apostles' days. This was the view of St. Ambrose, and also of Cajetan. It was reserved for Cardinal Bellarmine to expound 1 John i. 9 as only promising forgiveness if confession were made to a priest.

Sect. VI.—It may, however, be boldly said, that for many hundred years after Christ, the Fathers held no such views. Testimonies of Tertullian, of St. Cyprian, of Salvianus, of St. Ambrose, of Gennadius : all of whom speak of public confessions of sin, but not of auricular confession—a practice which Cardinal Bellarmine strives in vain to find in the writings of St. Cyprian.

Sect. VII.—The first of the Fathers to mention private confession is Origen. His words, however, relate to the practice which began to prevail, of choosing in the first place, one priest, with whom to take counsel, before public confession be made to the Church. He pleads for great care in the choice of such an adviser. But both kinds of confession, private or public, were solely with a view to the assignment of due penance for sins committed, and to the claiming of the sympathy and prayers of the Church. The testimonies of Gregory, Bishop of Nyssa, and others, to this effect.

Sect. VIII.—The change from public to private confession was first made by the Greek Church. The ground upon which this was done was, that it was not desirable to make confession of all sins in public. It was also affirmed that the Novatianists took occasion to insult the discipline of the Church, their own view being that no man ought to be readmitted to the Church, who was known to have offended after baptism.

Sect. IX.—The practice of the Greek Church, for about a hundred years, was that one presbyter in each congregation should receive the voluntary confessions of those who had sinned after baptism. But presently (after a grievous scandal in connection with a minister of the Church) it seemed good to Nectarius, Bishop of Constantinople, to abolish the office of penitentiary altogether. This change was soon adopted by other bishops everywhere.

Sect. X.—Examination of the charge brought against the truth of this story by Cardinal Baronius. He alleges that those who put it forth were themselves Novatianists; but this allegation can easily be disproved. Then he pretends that it was only public confession which Nectarius abolished; but this is wholly at variance with history. Public confessions had already been abolished by the first decree referred to in section viii.

Sect. XI.—Cardinal Bellarmine's attack upon the same story; his view being that the first establishment of penitentiaries in the Greek Church was only to meet the case of those who had publicly sinned after baptism; that such offenders were first to confess privately, then, by direction of the penitentiary, to make open confession and do public penance; and that whereas, before the Novatian schism, no one had been forced to confess publicly any sin, the original canon of the Greek Church made such, in the case of public offenders, compulsory, the decree of Nectarius only taking away this compulsion. But this view can very easily be disproved, by the express testimony of Sozomen, and of language used by Fabian, Bishop of Rome.

Sect. XII.—A third attack upon the story is that of Hassels of Louvain (1551), who alleges that it was only one particular confessor, or penitentiary, who was deposed from his office, the office itself not being abolished. But this also can be disproved, not only by the express words of Eudæmon, that people would now be left to their own consciences, but also by the complaints made of inconvenience that would in consequence ensue, and by the adoption in other dioceses of the change made by Nectarius.

Sect. XIII.—Why is it, it may be asked, that the Church of Rome is so loth to admit that auricular confession was abolished by Nectarius in the Greek Church? Obviously, because it would follow that the Greek Church did not hold confession as a sacrament ordained by Christ. But if any confession could be accounted sacramental in the Greek Church, it would be *public* confession (for this alone was followed by absolution); and public confession is now, in the Romish Church, abolished. The fact is, that the course of ancient penitential discipline did not imply any need of auricular confession. The testimony of St. Ambrose, St. Chrysostom, Cassian, and Prosper hereon. The extreme views of the Romish Church as to auricular confession, stated and condemned.

Sect. XIV.—The views of the Reformed Churches, on the same subject of Confession. French discipline admitted public confession, but not private. Testimony of Antoine de Chandieu (1534–91) hereon. The Bohemian Church acknowledges the benefit of public confession in notorious cases, but in no case compels it. As to private confession, all the Churches of Germany (including the Lutherans) admit it as beneficial for all men, but place the whole benefit of such a practice upon the assurance of God's pardon for sin, conveyed (made sure) to the individual upon due repentance, through the ministry of the Church.

Sect. XV.—The views of the Church of England upon the same subject. First, as to public confession. We have a general confession in our own daily services. Each man is able to supplement this with mental consideration of his own sins; and if true contrition accompany his devotions, he may make, in the same way, the general absolution his own. Next, as to private confession. The minister's power to absolve is admitted, and private confession is allowed, but not commanded. Testimony of Bishop Jewel hereon. The inconveniences and perils attending upon confession have in some sense caused it to be discouraged; but special provision is made for its use when necessary: (i.) in preparation for the holy Eucharist, (ii.) in anticipation of death. Views of St. Ambrose as to absolution administered in cases of late or death-bed repentance.

Sect. XVI.—The testimony of St. Chrysostom, clearly showing that private confession is by no means necessary, but that in special cases the aid of the pastor may well and profitably be sought.

CHAPTER V.

OF SATISFACTION.

Sect. I.—Having considered the subject of Confession, we now pass on (see chap. iii. sect. vi.) to that of Satisfaction. Definition of this term: "Whatsoever a penitent should do in the humbling himself before God, and testifying by deeds of contrition the same which confession in words pretendeth." The language of Tertullian, St. Chrysostom, St. Cyprian, and St. Augustine, fitting in with this definition. The phrase of John the Baptist, "works worthy of repentance" (Matt. iii. 8).

Sect. II.—The only Satisfaction, with regard to God Himself, is that made by Christ upon the cross. Faith and repentance necessary on man's part, before he can be fit to receive the benefits of His satisfaction. Our faith and repentance only to be termed satisfactory to God, inasmuch as His mercy requires no more at our hands.

Sect. III.—Repentance, the operation of God's grace within us; Satisfaction, the effect which it produces, either towards God or man. We satisfy, in doing that which is sufficient. Christ is the great High Priest, Who has made perfect satisfaction; but Christians are likewise priests (Rev. i. 6) to offer praise and thankfulness, whilst we continue in the way of life, and the sacrifice of a broken heart, when we fall into sin. In this sense, our repentance satisfies God.

Sect. IV.—And this it does, even though temporal chastisements are seen to follow upon sin. Illustrations from Old Testament history. Punishment after sin is not revenge, but is only sent for our amendment of life. St. Augustine's phrase: "Before forgiveness, they are punishment of sinners; after forgiveness, they are exercises and trials of righteous men."

Sect. V.—The virtue of repentance, consisting as it does of Contrition, Confession, and Satisfaction (see chap. iii. sect. v.), is therefore well spoken of in glowing terms, and with a wealth of illustration, as a "full restoration of the seat of grace and throne of glory," etc.

Sect. VI.—The three especial works of Satisfaction: Prayer, Fasts, and Almsdeeds. All of these have, in the performance of them, painfulness; and, in their nature, something opposite to sin. St. Cyprian's earnest words hereon; and Salvianus' caution that such works have no merit to buy out sin, but are only tokens of meek submission.

Sect. VII.—When we come to consider Satisfaction with regard to men, we find that often, repentance is of no effect without it. The law of the Jews especially rigid in this respect. The precepts in Leviticus vi., and the minute directions of Jewish Rabbis thereon.

Sect. VIII.—The ancient discipline, as shown by the canons of the primitive Church, was exceedingly careful that outward signs of contrition should be apparent in the offender, and full proof given of amendment of life. St. Basil mentions seven years of probation, in some instances, before readmission to Communion; the Nicene Synod, under Constantine, ordained, in some extreme cases, twelve years of such probation. This period, however, might be shortened, either if the penitent drew near to death, or if special circumstances justified such a course. The various stages of penitence, and the gradual approach to the full privileges of the Church. The practice of seeking for the intercession of martyrs, to shorten such periods of exclusion : St. Cyprian thereon, who clearly shows that no absolution, however obtained, can be valid without sufficient repentance.

Sect. IX.—The teaching of the Church of Rome, or "sacramental satisfaction." Wholly mistaking the end or object of Satisfaction, and wholly contrary to the order of the primitive Church, she has devised a theory that whilst eternal punishment is remitted by God, a certain amount of punishment in hell is allotted to men, which may be lessened or wholly done away with, by the merit of good works, either of themselves or others. The Pope's grant necessary, for the enjoyment of such privileges. " By this postern-gate cometh in the whole mart of papal indulgences . . . a scorn both to God and man."

CHAPTER VI.

OF ABSOLUTION OF PENITENTS.

Sect. I.—Absolution—what is meant thereby? It can only truly come from God (Matt. ix. 2). But as Nathan absolves David (2 Sam. xii. 13), so now the Apostles and ministers of Christ absolve sinners in His Name : not as prophets, but with the "certainty, partly of faith, and partly of human experience."

Sect. II.—The difference between ourselves and the Church of Rome, both as regards Repentance and Absolution. We insist upon the repentance of the heart; they upon "a sacramental penance of their own devising." We desire so to teach that a wounded soul "may learn the way how to cure itself"; their teaching is, "no cure without the priest." With ourselves, it is God who forgives, according to His gracious promises; with them, no absolution but from the priest.

Sect. III.—The two restraints, which our Lord has placed upon the authority of His ministers, in this respect: (i.) that the "practice proceed in due order"; (ii.) that it "do not extend itself beyond due bounds." Illustration from the history of Joseph, showing that the claim of Romish priests to be the sole dispensers of pardon, is absolutely untenable.

Sect. IV.—The force of Absolution—what it is. The Romish view, that it takes away sin. Our view, that it but makes us sure of God's gracious pardon. St. Cyprian on Matthew ix. 2: Christ the one Absolver—yet not so, but that the minister of Christ, in the right performance of his office, may declare forgiveness in His name.

Sect. V.—Two things necessary for remission of sins: grace, which takes away sin; repentance, as a condition required in us. The consoling power of Absolution: the approval by Christ's minister of our repentance, and his assurances of pardon in his Master's Name. This often sorely missed when the opportunity for it has been withdrawn. The double effect of Absolution: (i.) as regards our sins, it declares God's pardon; (ii.) as regards our use of Church privileges, it confirms us in the use of them with authority. The former, however, can only be held to mean a pronouncement concerning sinners, "according to that which may be gathered from outward signs"; to do more, is to do that which passes man's ability. The latter is absolute—a power committed by Christ Himself to His Church.

Sect. VI.—Opposition to this doctrine in the early Church. Tertullian: the bitterness and severity of his character. His view, that certain sins were incapable of forgiveness. Novatian holds the same opinion, and his followers frame a "bitter canon" to the effect that those who fall into deadly sin after baptism are never again to be admitted to the Communion. Sketch of Novatianist errors: they include second marriages in the number of unpardonable sins.

Sect. VII.—Absolution, in the Church of Rome, is too harshly enforced; and yet practically it amounts to a relaxation of discipline which has, for many, become a bare formality. And this Absolution being given, before works of satisfaction are imposed, these latter are simply works to be performed, or, it may be, remitted by indulgences from the Pope.

Contents

Sect. VIII.—We may estimate the true force and effect of Absolution by considering the threefold character of sin. There is, first, the act of sin; next, the stain or pollution of sin; and lastly, the punishment due to sin. The act of sin, God alone can remit, in that His purpose is never to call it to account; the stain of sin, He cleanses by His Holy Spirit; and from the punishment of sin, He alone can deliver. The ministerial sentence of private Absolution can, therefore, only declare that which God has done. Illustrations of this from the Old Testament, and from the writings of Peter Lombard and of St. Jerome.

Sect. IX.—The Romish Church has, however, forsaken such doctrine as this, and has advanced the discipline of repentance to the rank of a sacrament, of which Absolution is the outward sign. This it has done on the authority of a canon of the Council of Florence, which adopted the idea from Thomas Aquinas, forgetting that no sacrament can in itself work grace, and that grace can only come through the Divine presence in the ministry of the sacrament.

Sect. X.—Further expression of the view stated above. Cardinal Bellarmine has written much against the Protestant opinions as to sacramental grace, but has much misrepresented them. We do not look upon sacraments as empty signs, or teach that the only effect of them is Divine instruction; but just as we distinguish between the Divine and the human natures of our Lord, so we distinguish between the outward sign in a sacrament and the secret concurrence of God's Holy Spirit therewith. The elements, and the words used, may be called seals of God's truth; but only the Spirit, affixed to those elements and words, has power of operation within the soul. The views of Thomas Aquinas not implicitly followed by the Church of Rome, which now teaches that grace is an immediate effect of the outward sign, and that God's own motion gives efficacy thereto. Views of St. Cyprian in opposition to this modern view.

Sect. XI.—Thus the difference between the Protestant and Romish doctrine is, that we claim that to the outward sign God is pleased to join His Holy Spirit—a position which they cannot accept. The Councils of Florence and of Trent define that "sacraments contain and confer grace"; our doctrine is that the Holy Spirit works with, but not by, the outward sign. The agreement of the Protestant view, with that of the old schoolmen. The doctrine of the Church of England on this point, restated and illustrated.

Sect. XII.—Applying these principles to the so-called Sacrament of Penitence, it will be seen that the Romish teaching

Contents 25

amounts to this, that the ministry of the priest, and his Absolution, is a cause from which forgiveness proceeds as an effect. And yet abundant testimony is given, not only by their divines, but also by the Council of Trent, that any man who turns to God with his whole heart is at once forgiven, which would seem to be quite at variance with the teaching of the Romish Church, and to fit in exactly with the teaching of our Church.

Sect. XIII.—But to meet this difficulty, they have two answers ready. The one, that Absolution produces inward repentance, often absent from the mind of the so-called penitent ; the other, that penitents are only forgiven of God, in that they desire to receive Absolution from the priest. Examination and condemnation of both these as erroneous and absurd.

Sect. XIV.—The right use of Absolution. The testimony of men's conscience, concerning their own unforgiven sins, hard to bear. This observed even by infidels and heathens. Illustration, the Roman Emperor Tiberius. In such cases the help and guidance of the ministry is often most useful.

Sect. XV.—Let us take as an instance, the case of one who thinks that he has committed an unpardonable sin. Such a sin our Saviour mentions as possible (Mark iii. 29, 30). Examination of the meaning of this passage, which has often been misunderstood.

Sect. XVI.—Or again, the case of those who feel that their repentance is insufficient, their prayers cold, their fastings insufficient. To such, the timely and helpful counsels of wise ministers, speaking with authority in God's Name, may often bring peace and consolation. Such helps, though not laid of necessity upon any, can be forbidden to none.

Sect. XVII.—In conclusion, it should be urged that sincerity, not excitement, is the true measure of repentance. God looks at the heart, not at that which is outward. Comfortable words of St. Chrysostom and St. Augustine as to this : "Lord, in Thy book and volume of life all shall be written, as well the least of Thy saints as the chiefest."

THE SIXTH BOOK OF THE LAWS OF ECCLESIASTICAL POLITY.

CONTAINING THEIR FIFTH ASSERTION, THAT OUR LAWS ARE CORRUPT AND REPUGNANT TO THE LAWS OF GOD, IN MATTER BELONGING TO THE POWER OF ECCLESIASTICAL JURISDICTION, IN THAT WE HAVE NOT THROUGHOUT ALL CHURCHES CERTAIN LAY-ELDERS ESTABLISHED FOR THE EXERCISE OF THAT POWER.[1]

THE MATTER CONTAINED IN THIS SIXTH BOOK.

I. The question between us, whether all congregations or parishes ought to have lay-elders invested with power of jurisdiction in spiritual causes.
II. The nature of spiritual jurisdiction.
III. Of Penitency, the chiefest end propounded by spiritual jurisdiction. Two kinds of penitency; the one a private duty towards God, the other a duty of external discipline. Of the virtue of Repentance, from which the former duty proceedeth, and of Contrition, the first part of that duty.
IV. Of the discipline of Repentance instituted by Christ, practised by the Fathers, converted by the schoolmen into a sacrament; and of Confession, that which belongeth to the virtue of Repentance, that which was used among the Jews, that which papacy imagineth a sacrament, and that which ancient discipline practised.
V. Of Satisfaction.
VI. Of Absolution of Penitents.

CHAPTER I.

OUGHT LAY-ELDERS TO HAVE AUTHORITY IN SPIRITUAL CASES?

[1.] THE same men which in heat of contention do hardly either speak or give ear to reason, being

---

[1] The first and second chapters of this Book have undoubtedly reference to this subject. But when we come to chapter iii., we see that the writer passes away to that

after sharp and bitter conflicts retired[1] to a calm remembrance of all their former proceedings; the causes that brought them into quarrel, the course which their striving affections have followed, and the issue whereunto they are come, may peradventure, as troubled waters, in small time, of their own accord, by certain easy degrees settle themselves again, and so recover that clearness of well-advised judgment whereby they shall stand at the length indifferent both to yield and admit any reasonable satisfaction, where before they could not endure with patience to be gainsayed. Neither will I despair of the like success in these unpleasant controversies touching ecclesiastical polity; the time of silence,[2] which both parts have willingly taken to breathe, seeming now as it were a pledge of all men's quiet contentment to hear with more indifferency the weightiest and last remains of that cause, jurisdiction,[3] dignity,[4] dominion ecclesiastical.[5] For, let not any imagine, that the bare and naked difference of a few ceremonies could either have kindled so much fire, or have caused it to flame so long; but that the parties which herein laboured mightily for change and (as they say) for reformation, had somewhat more than this mark whereat to aim.

[2.] Having therefore drawn out a complete form, as they suppose, of public service to be done to God, and set down their plot for the office of the ministry in that behalf, they very well knew how little their labours so far forth bestowed would avail them in the end, without a claim of jurisdiction to uphold the fabric which they have erected; and this neither likely to be obtained but by the strong hand of the people, nor the people un-

which is indeed the proper subject matter of the Book, viz., Confession, Satisfaction, and Absolution. See the headings as printed on p. 27, "The matter contained in this Sixth Book."

[1] Retired: *i.e.* brought back again.

[2] It will be seen from the Introduction above, that the first four Books of the "Polity" were published in 1594; the fifth Book, in 1597. The remaining Books were completed, but not published, at the time of Hooker's death in 1600.

[3] Book vi. (original draught).
[4] Book vii.   [5] Book viii.

likely to favour it; the more, if overture were made of their own interest, right, and title thereunto. Whereupon there are many which have conjectured this to be the cause, why in all the projects of their discipline (it being manifest that their drift is to wrest the key of spiritual authority out of the hands of former governors, and equally to possess therewith the pastors of all several congregations) the people, first for surer accomplishment, and then for better defence thereof, are pretended [1] necessary actors in those things, whereunto their ability for the most part is as slender as their title and challenge unjust.

[3.] Notwithstanding (whether they saw it necessary for them to persuade the people, without whose help they could do nothing, or else, which I rather think, the affection which they bear towards this new form of government made them to imagine it God's own ordinance) their doctrine is, that, by the law of God, there must be for ever in all congregations certain lay-elders, ministers of ecclesiastical jurisdiction, inasmuch as our Lord and Saviour by testament (for so they presume) hath left all ministers or pastors in the Church executors equally to the whole power of spiritual jurisdiction, and with them hath joined the people as colleagues. By maintenance of which assertion there is unto that part apparently gained a twofold advantage, both because the people in this respect are much more easily drawn to favour it, as a matter of their own interest; and for that, if they chance to be crossed by such as oppose against them, the colour of divine authority, assumed for the grace and countenance of that power in the vulgar sort, furnisheth their leaders with great abundance of matter, behoveful for their encouragement to proceed always with hope of fortunate success in the end, considering their cause to be as David's was, a just defence of power given them from above, and consequently, their adversaries' quarrel the same with Saul's, by whom the ordinance of God was withstood.

[1] *i.e.* By the Puritan party. It was part of their plan to give some share of Church government to the laity. See Bancroft's Dangerous Positions, Book iv. chapter 12.

[4.] Now, on the contrary side, if their surmise prove false; if such,[1] as in justification whereof no evidence sufficient either hath been or can be alleged, (as I hope it shall clearly appear after due examination and trial,) let them consider whether those words of Korah, Dathan, and Abiram against Moses and against Aaron,[2] "It is too much that ye take upon you, seeing all the congregation is holy," be not the very true abstract and abridgment of all their published Admonitions, Demonstrations, Supplications, and Treatises whatsoever, whereby they have laboured to avoid[3] the rooms of their spiritual superiors before authorized, and to advance the new fancied sceptre of lay-presbyterial power.

CHAPTER II.

THE NATURE OF SPIRITUAL JURISDICTION.

[1.] But before there can be any settled determination, whether truth do rest on their part or on ours, touching lay-elders, we are to prepare the way thereunto by explication of some things requisite and very needful to be considered; as, first, how besides that spiritual power which is of order, and was instituted for performance of those duties whereof there hath been speech already had, there is in the Church no less necessary a second kind, which we call the power of jurisdiction. When the Apostle doth speak of ruling the Church of God, and of receiving accusations,[4] his words have evident reference to the power of jurisdiction. Our Saviour's words to the power of order, when he giveth his disciples charge, saying, "Preach: baptize: do this in remembrance of me."[5] A bishop (saith Ignatius) doth bear the image of God and of Christ; of God in ruling, of Christ in administering, holy things.[6] By this there-

---

[1] The sentence is somewhat involved. But the construction would seem to be, "If such (views are erroneous)," etc.
[2] Num. xvi. 3.
[3] Avoid: *i.e.* make empty.
[4] Acts xx. 28; 1 Tim. v. 19.

[5] Mark xvi. 15; Matt. xxviii. 19; 1 Cor. xi. 24.
[6] Τίμα μὲν τὸν Θεὸν, ὡς αἴτιον τῶν ὅλων καὶ κύριον. Ἐπίσκοπον δὲ, ὡς ἀρχιερέα, Θεοῦ εἰκόνα φοροῦντα· κατὰ μὲν τὸ ἄρχειν, Θεοῦ, κατὰ δὲ τὸ ἱερατεύειν Χριστοῦ. Epist. ad Smyrn. [c. 9.].

fore we see a manifest difference acknowledged between the power of ecclesiastical order, and the power of jurisdiction ecclesiastical.

[2.] The spiritual power of the Church being such as neither can be challenged by right of nature, nor could by human authority be instituted, because the forces and effects thereof are supernatural and divine, we are to make no doubt or question but that from him which is the Head it hath descended unto us that are the body now invested therewith. He gave it for the benefit and good of souls, as a mean to keep them in the path which leadeth unto endless felicity, a bridle to hold them within their due and convenient bounds, and, if they do go astray, a forcible help to reclaim them. Now although there be no kind of spiritual power, for which our Lord Jesus Christ did not give both commission to exercise and direction how to use the same; although his laws in that behalf, recorded by the holy evangelists, be the only ground and foundation whereupon the practice of the Church must sustain itself; yet, as all multitudes, once grown to the form of societies, are even thereby naturally warranted to enforce upon their own subjects particularly those things which public wisdom shall judge expedient for the common good; so it were absurd to imagine the Church itself, the most glorious amongst them, abridged of this liberty, or to think that no law, constitution, or canon, can be further made either for limitation or amplification in the practice of our Saviour's ordinances, whatsoever occasion be offered through variety of times and things, during the state of this inconstant world, which bringeth forth daily such new evils as must of necessity by new remedies be redressed, and did both of old enforce our venerable predecessors, and will always constrain others, sometime to make, sometime to abrogate, sometime to augment, and again to abridge sometime; in sum, often to vary, alter, and change customs incident unto the manner of exercising that power which doth itself continue always one and the same. I therefore conclude that spiritual authority is a power which Christ hath given to be used over them which are subject unto it for the eternal good of their souls, according to his own most sacred laws and the wholesome positive constitutions of his Church.

[1] In doctrine referred unto action and practice, as this is which concerns spiritual jurisdiction, the first sound and perfect understanding is the knowledge of the end, because thereby both use doth frame, and contemplation judge, all things.

CHAPTER III.
OF PENITENCE.

[1.] Seeing that the chiefest cause of spiritual jurisdiction is to provide for the health and safety of men's souls, by bringing them to see and repent their grievous offences committed against God, as also to reform all injuries offered with the breach of Christian love and charity towards their brethren in matters of ecclesiastical cognizance;[2] the use of this power shall by so much the plainlier appear, if first the nature of repentance itself be known.

---

[1] At this point, we may refer our readers to the Introduction, in which the history of the Sixth Book is noted at some length. The learned editors of the latest edition of Hooker's works (Dean Church and Canon Paget) are of opinion that the point of transition from the original draft of the Sixth Book, to the treatise upon Penitence, is to be found at the words, "The virtue of repentance in the heart of man," etc. (§ 2 on page 34)—"if not before." May the present editor be permitted to conjecture, that the point of transition is more likely to be at the words, "We are by repentance, etc.," a few lines below, and that the paragraphs "In doctrine referred," etc., and the opening sentences of chapter iii., are the somewhat strained connection, from the pen of the original editor, between the opening of a treatise upon Lay Government, and the main body of another treatise upon Penitence?

[2] This clause ("in matters of ecclesiastical cognizance") is, as the edition of Dean Church and Canon Paget points out, "no doubt inserted with especial purpose of qualifying the general expression before, of 'reforming all injuries,' etc., and so avoiding the claim of extreme prerogative, which the Puritans urged in order to draw all cases into their spiritual courts." In future notes from the edition above named, I shall acknowledge them by the reference "C. and P."

Repentance, the Effect of Divine Grace

We are by repentance to appease whom we offend by sin. For which cause, whereas all sin deprives us of the favour of Almighty God, our way of reconciliation with him is the inward secret repentance of the heart; which inward repentance alone sufficeth, unless some special thing, in the quality of sin committed, or in the party that hath done amiss, require more. For besides our submission in God's sight, repentance must not only proceed to the private contentation [1] of men, if the sin be a crime injurious; but also further, where the wholesome discipline of God's Church exacteth a more exemplary and open satisfaction.[2] Now the Church being satisfied with outward repentance, as God is with inward, it shall not be amiss, for more perspicuity, to term this latter always the virtue, the former the discipline of repentance: which discipline hath two sorts of penitents to work upon, inasmuch as it hath been accustomed to lay the offices of repentance on some seeking, others shunning them; on some at their own voluntary request, on others altogether against their wills, as shall hereafter appear by store of ancient examples. Repentance being, therefore, either in the sight of God alone, or else with the notice also of men: without the one,[3] sometimes thoroughly performed, but always practised more or less in our daily devotions and prayers, we can have no remedy for any fault; whereas the other [4] is only required in sins of a certain degree and quality: the one necessary for ever, the other so far forth as the laws and order of God's Church shall make it requisite. The

---

[1] Contentation: *i.e.* satisfying the claims of men, or making reparation to them.

[2] Pœnitentiæ secundæ, et unius, quanto in actu negotium est, tanto potior probatio est, ut non sola conscientia proferatur, sed aliquo etiam actu administretur." "Second penitency, following that before baptism, and being not more than once admitted in one man, requireth by so much the greater labour to make it manifest, for that it is not a work which can come again in trial, but must be therefore with some open solemnity executed, and not left to be discharged with the privity of conscience alone." Tertull. de Pœnit. [c. 9].

[3] *i.e.* repentance in the sight of God.

[4] *i.e.* repentance with the notice of men.

nature, parts, and effects of the one always the same; the other limited, extended, and varied by infinite occasions.

[2.] The virtue of repentance in the heart of man is God's handy-work, a fruit or effect of divine grace, which grace continually offereth itself even unto them that have forsaken it, as may appear by the words of Christ in St. John's Revelation,[1] "I stand at the door and knock": nor doth he only knock without, but also within assist to open, whereby access and entrance is given to the heavenly presence of that saving power, which maketh man a repaired temple for God's good Spirit again to inhabit. And albeit the whole train of virtues which are implied in the name of grace be infused at one instant; yet because, when they meet and concur unto any effect in man, they have their distinct operations rising orderly one from another, it is no unnecessary thing that we note the way or method of the Holy Ghost in framing man's sinful heart to repentance. A work, the first foundation whereof is laid by opening and illuminating the eye of faith, because by faith are discovered the principles of this action, whereunto, unless the understanding do first assent, there can follow in the will towards penitency no inclination at all. Contrariwise, the resurrection of the dead, the judgment of the world to come, and the endless misery of sinners, being apprehended, this worketh fear; such as theirs was who, feeling their own distress and perplexity in that passion, besought our Lord's Apostles earnestly to give them counsel what they should do.[2] For fear is impotent and unable to advise itself; yet this good it hath, that men are thereby made desirous to prevent, if possibly they may, whatsoever evil they dread. The first thing that wrought the Ninevites' repentance, was fear of destruction within forty days:[3] signs and miraculous works of God, being extraordinary representations of divine power, are commonly wont to stir any the most wicked with terror, lest the same power should bend itself against them.

[1] Rev. iii. 20.   [2] Acts ii. 37.   [3] Jonah iii. 5.

And because tractable minds, though guilty of much sin, are hereby moved to forsake those evil ways which make his power in such sort their astonishment and fear, therefore our Saviour denounced his curse against Chorazin and Bethsaida, saying, that, if Tyre and Sidon had seen that which they did, those signs which prevailed little with the one would have brought the others to repentance.[1] As the like thereunto did in the men given to curious arts, of whom the apostolic history saith,[2] that "fear came upon them, and many which had followed vain sciences burnt openly the very books out of which they had learned the same." As fear of contumely and disgrace amongst men, together with other civil punishments, are a bridle to restrain from any heinous acts whereinto men's outrage would otherwise break; so the fear of divine revenge and punishment, where it takes place, doth make men desirous to be rid likewise from that inward guiltiness of sin wherein they would else securely continue.

[3.] Howbeit, when faith has wrought a fear of the event of sin, yet repentance hereupon ensueth not, unless our belief conceive both the possibility and means to avert evil; the possibility, inasmuch as God is merciful and most willing to have sin cured; the means, because he hath plainly taught what is requisite and shall suffice unto that purpose. The nature of all wicked men is, for fear of revenge to hate whom they most wrong; the nature of hatred, to wish that destroyed which it cannot brook; and from hence arise the furious endeavours of godless and obdurate sinners to extinguish in themselves the opinion of God, because they would not have him to be, whom execution of endless woe doth not suffer them to love.

Every sin against God abateth, and continuance in sin extinguisheth, our love towards him. It was therefore said to the angel of Ephesus, having sinned,[3] "Thou art fallen away from thy first love"; so that, as we never decay in love till we sin, in like sort neither can we possibly forsake sin, unless we first begin again to love.

---
[1] St. Matt. xi. 21.   [2] Acts xix. 17, 19.   [3] Rev. ii. 5.

Ch. III. § 3. What is love towards God, but a desire of union with God? And shall we imagine a sinner converting himself to God, in whom there is no desire of union with God presupposed? I therefore conclude, that fear worketh no man's inclination to repentance, till somewhat else have wrought in us love also; our love and desire of union with God ariseth from the strong conceit which we have of his admirable goodness; the goodness of God which particularly moveth unto repentance is, his mercy towards mankind, notwithstanding sin: for, let it once sink deeply into the mind of man, that howsoever we have injured God, his very nature is averse from revenge, except unto sin we add obstinacy, otherwise always ready to accept our submission as a full discharge or recompense for all wrongs; and can we choose but begin to love him whom we have offended? or can we but begin to grieve that we have offended him whom we love? Repentance considereth sin as a breach of the law of God, an act obnoxious [1] to that revenge, which notwithstanding may be prevented if we pacify God in time.

The root and beginning of penitency, therefore, is the consideration of our own sin, as a cause which hath procured the wrath, and a subject which doth need the mercy, of God. For unto man's understanding there being presented, on the one side, tribulation and anguish upon every soul that doth evil; on the other, eternal life unto them which by continuance in well-doing seek glory, and honour, and immortality: on the one hand, a curse to the children of disobedience; on the other, to lovers of righteousness all grace and benediction: yet between these extremes that eternal God, from whose unspotted justice and undeserved mercy the lot of each inheritance proceedeth, is so inclinable rather to shew compassion than to take revenge, that all his speeches in holy Scripture are almost nothing else but entreaties of men to prevent destruction by amendment of their wicked lives; all the works of his providence little other than mere allurements of the just to continue stedfast,

---

[1] Obnoxious: *i.e.* liable.

and of the unrighteous to change their course; all his dealings and proceedings towards true converts, as have even filled the grave writings of holy men with these and the like most sweet sentences:[1] "Repentance (if I may so speak) stoppeth God in his way, when being provoked by crimes past he cometh to revenge them with most just punishments; yea, it tieth as it were the hands of the avenger, and doth not suffer him to have his will." Again,[2] "The merciful eye of God towards men hath no power to withstand penitency, at what time soever it comes in presence." And again, "God doth not take it so in evil part, though we wound that which he hath required us to keep whole, as that after we have taken hurt there should be in us no desire to receive his help." Finally, lest I be carried too far in so large a sea, "There was never any man condemned of God but for neglect, nor justified except he had care, of repentance."

[4.] From these considerations, setting before our eyes our inexcusable both unthankfulness in disobeying so merciful, foolishness in provoking so powerful a God, there ariseth necessarily a pensive and corrosive desire that we had done otherwise; a desire which suffereth us to foreslow no time,[3] to feel no quietness within ourselves, to take neither sleep nor food with contentment, never to give over supplications, confessions, and other penitent duties, till the light of God's reconciled favour shine in our darkened soul.

Fulgentius asking the question,[4] why David's confession should be held for effectual penitence, and not Saul's? answereth, that the one hated sin, the other feared only punishment in this world: Saul's acknow-

---

[1] Cassian. Col. 20, ch. v.
[2] Basil. Epist. Seleuc. p. 106. Φιλάνθρωπον βλέμμα προσιοῦσαν αἰδεῖται μετάνοιαν. Chr. in 1 Cor. Hom. 8. Οὐ τὸ τρωθῆναι οὕτω δεινὸν, ὡς τὸ τρωθέντα μὴ βούλεσθαι θεραπεύεσθαι. Marc. Erem. Οὐδεὶς κατεκρίθη, εἰ μὴ μετανοίας κατεφρόνησε, καὶ οὐδεὶς ἐδικαιώθη, εἰ μὴ ταύτης ἐπεμελήσατο. [De Pœnit. p. 915, vol i. Bibliotheca. Patr. Græc. ed. Par. 1624.]
[3] To foreslow no time: *i.e.* to make no delay.
[4] Fulg. de Remis. Peccat. lib. ii. cap. 15.

ledgment of sin was fear; David's, both fear and also love.

This was the fountain of Peter's tears, this the life and spirit of David's eloquence, in those most admirable hymns entitled Penitential, where the words of sorrow for sin do melt the very bowels of God remitting it; and the comforts of grace in remitting sin carry him which sorrowed rapt as it were into heaven, with ecstasies of joy and gladness. The first motive of the Ninevites unto repentance, was their belief in a sermon of fear, but the next and most immediate, an axiom of love;[1] "Who can tell whether God will turn away his fierce wrath, that we perish not?" No conclusion such as theirs, " Let every man turn from his evil way," but out of premises such as theirs were, fear and love. Wherefore the well-spring of repentance is faith, first breeding fear, and then love; which love causes hope, hope resolution of attempt;[2] " I will go to my Father, and say, I have sinned against heaven, and against thee "; that is to say, I will do what the duty of a convert requireth.

[5.] Now in a penitent's or a convert's duty there are included, first, the aversion[3] of the will from sin; secondly, the submission of ourselves to God by supplication and prayer; thirdly, the purpose of a new life, testified with present works of amendment : which three things do very well seem to be comprised in one definition by them which handle repentance, as a virtue that hateth, bewaileth, and showeth a purpose to amend sin. We offend God in thought, word, and deed: to the first of which three, they make contrition; to the second, confession ; and to the last, our works of satisfaction, answerable.[4]

Contrition doth not here import those sudden pangs and convulsions of the mind which cause sometimes the most forsaken of God to retract their own doings; it is no natural passion, or anguish, which riseth in us against our wills, but a deliberate aversion of the will of man

---

[1] Jonah iii. 9. [2] Luke xv. 18. [4] Answerable : *i.e.* to correspond.
[3] Aversion : *i.e.* turning away.

from sin; which being always accompanied with grief, and grief oftentimes partly with tears, partly with other external signs, it hath been thought that in these things contrition doth chiefly consist: whereas the chiefest thing in contrition is, that alteration whereby the will, which was before delighted with sin, doth now abhor and shun nothing more. But forasmuch as we cannot hate sin in ourselves without heaviness and grief, that there should be in us a thing of such hateful quality, the will averted from sin must needs make the affection suitable; yea, there is great reason why it should so do: for since the will by conceiving sin hath deprived the soul of life, and of life there is no recovery without repentance, the death of sin; repentance not able to kill sin, but by withdrawing the will from it; the will unpossible to be withdrawn, unless it concur with a contrary affection to that which accompanied it before in evil; is it not clear that as an inordinate delight did first begin sin, so repentance must begin with a just sorrow, a sorrow of heart, and such a sorrow as renteth[1] the heart; neither a feigned nor a slight sorrow; not feigned, lest it increase sin, nor slight, lest the pleasures of sin overmatch it?

[6.] Wherefore of grace, the highest cause from which man's penitency doth proceed; of faith, fear, love, hope, what force and efficiency they have in repentance; of parts and duties thereunto belonging, comprehended in the schoolmen's definitions; finally, of the first among those duties, contrition, which disliketh and bewaileth iniquity, let this suffice.

And because God will have offences by repentance not only abhorred within ourselves, but also with humble supplication displayed before him, and a testimony of amendment to be given, even by present works worthy repentance, in that they are contrary to those we renounce and disclaim; although the virtue of repentance do require that her other two parts, confession and satisfaction, should here follow; yet seeing they belong as well to the discipline as to the virtue of

---

[1] Renteth: *i.e.* rendeth.

repentance, and only differ for that in the one they are performed to man, in the other to God alone I had rather distinguish them in joint-handling, than handle them apart, because in quality and manner of practice they are distinct.

CHAPTER IV.

OF REPENTANCE, AND OF CONFESSION.

[1]. Our Lord and Saviour in the sixteenth of St. Matthew's gospel giveth his Apostles regiment[1] in general over God's Church.[2] For they that have the keys of the kingdom of heaven are thereby signified to be stewards of the house of God, under whom they guide, command, judge, and correct his family. The souls of men are God's treasure, committed to the trust and fidelity of such as must render a strict account for the very least which is under their custody. God hath not invested them with power to make a revenue thereof, but to use it for the good of them whom Jesus Christ hath most dearly bought.

And because their office therein consisteth of sundry functions, some belonging to doctrine, some to discipline, all contained in the name of the Keys; they have for matters of discipline, as well litigious as criminal, their courts and consistories erected by the heavenly authority of his most sacred voice, who hath said, *Dic Ecclesiæ*,[3] Tell the Church; against rebellious and contumacious persons which refuse to obey their sentence, armed they are[4] with power to eject such out of the Church, to deprive them of the honours, rights, and privileges of Christian men, to make them as heathens and publicans, with whom society was hateful.

Furthermore, lest their acts should be slenderly accounted of, or had in contempt, whether they admit to the fellowship of saints or seclude from it, whether they bind offenders or set them again at liberty, whether they remit or retain sins, whatsoever is done by way of

---

[1] Regiment: *i.e.* rule.
[2] Matt. xvi. 19.
[3] Matt. xviii. 17.
[4] *i.e.* they are armed.

Of public Voluntary Confession 41

orderly and lawful proceeding, the Lord himself hath promised to ratify. This is that grand original warrant, by force whereof the guides and prelates in God's Church, first his Apostles, and afterwards others following them successively, did both use and uphold that discipline, the end whereof is to heal men's consciences, to cure their sins, to reclaim offenders from iniquity, and to make them by repentance just.[1]

Neither hath it of ancient time, for any other respect, been accustomed to bind by ecclesiastical censures, to retain so bound till tokens of manifest repentance appeared, and upon apparent repentance to release, saving only because this was received as a most expedient method for the cure of sin.

[2.] The course of discipline in former ages reformed open transgressors by putting them into offices of open penitence, especially confession, whereby they declared their own crimes in the hearing of the whole Church, and were not from the time of their first convention [2] capable of the holy mysteries of Christ till they had solemnly discharged this duty.

Offenders in secret knowing themselves altogether as unworthy to be admitted to the Lord's table, as the others which were withheld; being also persuaded, that if the Church did direct them in the offices of their penitency, and assist them with public prayers, they should more easily obtain that they sought, than by trusting wholly to their own endeavours; finally, having no impediment to stay them from it but bashfulness, which countervailed not the former inducements, and besides was greatly eased by the good construction which the charity of those times gave to such actions, wherein men's piety and voluntary care to be reconciled to God did purchase them much more love than their faults (the testimonies of common frailty) were able to

---

[1] Matt. xviii. 18; John xx. 23; 1 Cor. v. 3; 2 Cor. ii. 6; 1 Tim. i. 20.
[2] Convention: *i.e.* coming together; interview between the penitents and the officers of the Church.

procure disgrace, they made it not nice to use[1] some one of the ministers of God, by whom the rest might take notice of their faults, prescribe them convenient remedies, and in the end, after public confession, all join in prayer unto God for them.

[3.] The first beginner of this custom had the more followers, by means of that special favour which always was with good consideration shewed towards voluntary penitents above the rest.

But as professors of Christian belief grew more in number, so they waxed worse; when kings and princes had submitted their dominions unto the sceptre of Jesus Christ, by means whereof persecution ceasing, the Church immediately became subject to those evils which peace and security bringeth forth; there was not now that love which before kept all things in tune, but everywhere schisms, discords, dissensions amongst men, conventicles of heretics, bent more vehemently against the sounder and better sorts than very infidels and heathens themselves; faults not corrected in charity, but noted with delight, and kept for malice to use when the deadliest opportunities should be offered.

Whereupon, forasmuch as public confessions became dangerous and prejudicial to the safety of well-minded men, and in divers respects advantageous to the enemies of God's Church, it seemed first unto some, and afterwards generally, requisite, that voluntary penitents should surcease from open confession.

Instead whereof, when once private and secret confession had taken place with the Latins, it continued as a profitable ordinance, till the Lateran council had decreed[2] that all men once in a year at the least should confess themselves to the priest. So that being a thing thus made both general and also necessary, the next degree

---

[1] Made it not nice to use: *i.e.* had no hesitation in using. Cf. Shakespeare, King John, iii. 4:—
"He that stands upon a slippery place
Makes nice of no vile hold to stay him up."

[2] The 21st Canon of the 4th Lateran Council, held under Pope Innocent III. A.D. 1215. [C. and P.]

Of Sacramental Confession 43

of estimation whereunto it grew, was to be honoured and lifted up to the nature of a sacrament; that as Christ did institute Baptism to give life, and the Eucharist to nourish life, so Penitency might be thought a sacrament ordained to recover life, and Confession a part of the sacrament.

They define therefore their private penitency[1] to be a sacrament of remitting sins after baptism: the virtue of repentance, a detestation of wickedness with full purpose to amend the same, and with hope to obtain pardon at God's hands.

Wheresoever the Prophets cry *Repent*, and in the Gospel Saint Peter maketh the same exhortation to the Jews as yet unbaptized,[2] they would have the virtue of repentance only to be understood; the sacrament, where he adviseth Simon Magus to repent,[3] because the sin of Simon Magus was after baptism.

Now although they have only external repentance for a sacrament, internal for a virtue, yet make they sacramental repentance nevertheless to be composed of three parts, contrition, confession, and satisfaction. Which is absurd; because contrition, being an inward thing, belongeth to the virtue and not to the sacrament of repentance, which must consist of external parts, if the nature thereof be external. Besides, which is more absurd, they leave out absolution, whereas some of their school-divines,[4] handling penance in the nature of a sacrament, and being not able to espy the least resemblance of a sacrament save only in absolution, (for a sacrament by their doctrine must both signify and also confer or bestow some special divine grace,) resolved themselves, that the duties of the penitent could be but mere preparations to the sacrament, and that the sacrament itself was wholly in absolution. And albeit Thomas[5] with his followers have thought it safer to maintain, as

---

[1] The words are those of Soto, a Spanish Dominican, 1494–1560. [C. and P.: who give the Latin originals of both definitions.]

[2] Acts ii. 38.
[3] Acts viii. 22.
[4] Duns Scotus. See Appendix.
[5] *i.e.* Thomas Aquinas, 1596.

well the services of the penitent, as the words of the minister, necessary unto the essence of their sacrament; the services of the penitent, as a cause material; the words of absolution, as a formal, for that by them all things else are perfected to the taking away of sin; which opinion now reigneth in all their schools, since the time that the council of Trent[1] gave it solemn approbation, seeing they all make absolution, if not the whole essence, yet the very form whereunto they ascribe chiefly the whole force and operation of their sacrament; surely to admit the matter as a part, and not to admit the form, hath small congruity with reason.

Again, forasmuch as a sacrament is complete, having the matter and form which it ought, what should lead them to set down any other parts of sacramental repentance, than confession and absolution, as Durandus hath done?[2]

For, touching satisfaction, the end thereof, as they understand it, is a further matter which resteth after the sacrament administered, and therefore can be no part of the sacrament.

Will they draw in contrition with satisfaction, which are no parts, and exclude absolution, (a principal part,) yea, the very complement, form, and perfection of the rest, as themselves account it?

[4.] But for their breach of precepts in art it skilleth not, if their doctrine otherwise concerning penitency, and in penitency touching confession, might be found true.

We say, let no man look for pardon, which doth smother and conceal sin where in duty it should be revealed.

The cause why God requireth confession to be made to him is, that thereby testifying a deep hatred of our

---

[1] Sess. xiv. c. 3. "Docet sancta synodus sacramenti pœnitentiæ formam, in qua præcipue ipsius vis sita est, in illis ministri verbis positam esse, *Ego te Absolvo*. Sunt autem quasi materia hujus sacramenti ipsius pœnitentis actus, nempe contritio, confessio, et satisfactio."

[2] In iv. Sent. d. xvi. q. 164. [C. and P.]

Of Confession 45

own iniquity, the only cause of his hatred and wrath towards us, we might, because we are humble, be so much the more capable of that compassion and tender mercy which knoweth not how to condemn sinners that condemn themselves.

If it be our Saviour's own principle, that the conceit we have of our debt forgiven, proportioneth our thankfulness and love to him at whose hands we receive pardon;[1] doth not God foresee that they which with ill-advised modesty seek to hide their sin like Adam, that they which rake it up under ashes, and confess it not, are very unlikely to requite with offices of love afterwards the grace which they show themselves unwilling to prize at the very time when they sue for it; inasmuch as their not confessing what crimes they have committed is a plain signification how loth they are that the benefit of God's most gracious pardon should seem great? Nothing more true than that of Tertullian,[2] "Confession doth as much abate the weight of men's offences, as concealment doth make them heavier. For he which confesseth hath purpose to appease God; he, a determination to persist and continue obstinate, which keeps them secret to himself." St. Chrysostom, almost in the same words, "Wickedness is by being acknowledged lessened, and doth but grow by being hid. If men having done amiss let it slip, as though they knew no such matter, what is there to stay them from falling into one and the same evil? To call ourselves sinners availeth nothing, except we lay our faults in the balance, and take the weight of them one by one. Confess thy crimes to God, disclose thy transgressions before thy Judge, by way of humble supplication and suit, if not with tongue, at the least with heart, and in this sort seek mercy. A general persuasion that thou art a sinner will neither so humble nor bridle thy soul, as if the catalogue of thy sins examined severally be con-

---

[1] Luke vii. 47.
[2] "Tantum relevat confessio delictorum, quantum dissimulatio exaggerat. Confessio enim satisfactionis consilium est, dissimulatio contumaciæ." Tertull. de Pœnit. [c. 8 fin.].

Ch. iv. § 4. tinually kept in mind. This shall make thee lowly in thine own eyes; this shall preserve thy feet from falling, and sharpen thy desires towards all good things. The mind, I know, doth hardly admit such unpleasant remembrances; but we must force it, we must constrain it thereunto. It is safer now to be bitten with the memory, than hereafter with the torment of sin."[1]

The Jews, with whom no repentance for sin is available without confession, either conceived in mind or uttered, (which latter kind they call usually confession delivered by word of mouth,)[2] had first that general confession which once every year was made both severally by each of the people for himself upon the day of expiation, and by the priest for them all.[3] On the day of expiation the high-priest maketh three express confessions, acknowledging unto God the manifold transgressions of the whole nation, his own personal offences likewise, together with the sins, as well of his family as of the rest of his rank and order.

They had again their voluntary confessions, at the times and seasons when men, bethinking themselves of their wicked conversation past, were resolved to change their course, the beginning of which alteration was still confession of sins.

Thirdly, over and besides these, the law imposed upon them also that special confession, which they call confession of that particular fault for which we namely[4] seek pardon at God's hands.[5]

The words of the law concerning confession in this kind are as followeth: "When a man or woman shall commit any sin that men commit, and transgress against the Lord, their sin which they have done (that is to say, the very deed itself in particular) they shall acknowledge."[6]

In Leviticus, after certain transgressions there men-

---

[1] Homily xxx. on Epistle to the Hebrews.
[2] Lev. xvi. 21 : Heb. וְדוּי.
[3] "All Israel is bound on the day of expiation to repent and confess." R. Mos. in lib. Mitsuoth haggadol. par. 2, præ. 16.
[4] Namely : *i.e.* by name.
[5] Heb. וִדּוּי עַל עָוֹן מְיוּחָד.
[6] Num. v. 6.

Of the Virtue of Confession 47

tioned, we read the like: "When a man hath sinned in any one of these things, he shall then confess, how in that thing he hath offended."[1] For such kind of special sins they had also special sacrifices; wherein the manner was, that the offender should lay his hands on the head of the sacrifice which he brought, and should there make confession to God, saying,[2] "Now, O Lord, that I have offended, committed sin, and done wickedly in thy sight, this or this being my fault; behold I repent me, and am utterly ashamed of my doings; my purpose is, never to return more to the same crime."

"None of them, whom either the house of judgment had condemned to die, or of them which are to be punished with stripes, can be clear by being executed or scourged, till they repent and confess their faults."

Finally, there was no man amongst them at any time, either condemned to suffer death, or corrected, or chastised with stripes, none ever sick and near his end, but they called upon him to repent and confess his sins.[3]

Of malefactors convict by witnesses, and thereupon either adjudged to die, or otherwise chastised, their custom was to exact, as Joshua did of Achan, open confession:[4] "My son, now give glory to the Lord God of Israel; confess unto him, and declare unto me what thou hast committed: conceal it not from me."

Concerning injuries and trespasses, which happen between men, they highly commend such as will acknowledge before many. [5] "It is in him which "repenteth accepted as a high sacrifice, if he will confess "before many, make them acquainted with his over- "sights, and reveal the transgressions which have passed "between him and any of his brethren; saying, I have "verily offended this man, thus and thus I have done "unto him; but behold I do now repent and am sorry.

---

[1] Lev. v. 5.
[2] Misne Tora, Tractatu Teshuba, cap. 1: et R.M. in lib. Misnoth. par. 2. cap. 6.
[3] "To him which is sick and draweth towards death, they say, Confess." Mos. In Misnoth. par. 2, præ. 16.
[4] Josh. vii. 19.
[5] Maimonid. in Tract. Teshuboth. c. ii. § 6. [C. and P.]

Ch. iv. § 5. "Contrariwise, whosoever is proud, and will not be "known of his faults, but cloaketh them, is not yet "come to perfect repentance; for so it is written,[1] 'He "that hides his sins shall not prosper':" which words of Solomon they do not further extend than only to sins committed against men, which are in that respect meet before men to be acknowledged particularly. "But in sins between man and God, there is no necessity that man should himself make any such open and particular recital of them"; to God they are known, and of us it is required, that we cast not the memory of them carelessly and loosely behind our backs, but keep in mind, as near as we can, both our own debt, and his grace which remitteth the same.

[5.] Wherefore, to let pass Jewish confession, and to come unto them which hold confession in the ear of the priest commanded, yea, commanded in the nature of a sacrament, and thereby so necessary that sin without it cannot be pardoned; let them find such a commandment in holy Scripture, and we ask no more.

John the Baptist was an extraordinary person; his birth, his actions of life, his office extraordinary. It is therefore recorded for the strangeness of the act, but not set down as an everlasting law for the world, that to him Jerusalem and all Judea made confession of their sins;[2] besides, at the time of this confession, their pretended sacrament of repentance, as they grant, was not yet instituted; neither was it sin after baptism, which penitents did there confess. When that which befell the seven sons of Sceva, for using the name of our Lord Jesus Christ in their conjurations, was notified to Jews and Grecians in Ephesus,[3] it brought a universal fear upon them, insomuch that divers of them, which had believed before, but not obeyed the laws of Christ, as they should have done, being terrified by this example, came to the Apostle, and confessed their wicked deeds. Which good and virtuous act no wise man, as I suppose, will disallow, but commend highly in them, whom God's

---

[1] Prov. xxviii. 13.   [2] Matt. iii. 6.   [3] Acts xix. 18.

good Spirit shall move to do the like when need requireth. Yet neither hath this example the force of any general commandment or law, to make it necessary for every man to pour into the ears of the priest whatsoever hath been done amiss, or else to remain everlastingly culpable and guilty of sin; in a word, it proveth confession practised as a virtuous act, but not commanded as a sacrament.

Now concerning St. James's exhortation, whether the former branch be considered, which said,[1] "Is any sick among you? let him call for the ancients of the Church, and let them make their prayers for him"; or the latter, which stirreth up all Christian men unto mutual acknowledgment of faults amongst themselves, "Lay open your minds, make your confessions one to another"; is it not plain, that the one hath relation to that gift of healing, which our Saviour promised his Church, saying,[2] "They shall lay their hands on the sick, and the sick shall recover health"; relation to that gift of healing, whereby the Apostle imposed his hands on the father of Publius,[3] and made him miraculously a sound man; relation, finally, to that gift of healing, which so long continued in practice after the Apostles' times; that whereas the Novatianists denied the power of the Church of God in curing sin after baptism, St. Ambrose asked them again,[4] "Why it might not as well prevail with God for spiritual as for corporal and bodily health; yea, wherefore (saith he) do ye yourselves lay hands on the diseased, and believe it to be a work of benediction or prayer, if haply the sick person be restored to his former safety?" And of the other member, which toucheth mutual confession, do not some of themselves, as namely Cajetan,[5] deny that any other confession is meant, than only that "which seeketh either association of prayers, or reconciliation, or pardon of wrongs?" Is it not confessed by the greatest part of their own

---

[1] Jas. v. 14, 16. [2] Mark xvi. 18.
[3] Acts xxviii. 8.
[4] Ambros de Pœnitentia, lib. i. c. 8.
[5] Cajetan *in loco*. "Non hic est sermo de confessione sacramentali."

retinue,[1] that we cannot certainly affirm sacramental confession to have been meant or spoken of in this place? Howbeit, Bellarmine,[2] delighted to run a course by himself where colourable shifts of wit will but make the way passable, standeth as formally for this place, and not less for that in St. John than for this. St. John saith,[3] "If we confess our sins, God is faithful and just to forgive us our sins, and to cleanse us from all unrighteousness": doth St. John say, If we confess to the priest, God is righteous to forgive; and, if not, that our sins are unpardonable? No, but the titles of God, *just* and *righteous*, do import that he pardoneth sin only for his promise sake; "And there is not (they say) any promise of forgiveness upon confession made to God without the priest"; not any promise, but with this condition, and yet this condition nowhere expressed.

Is it not strange, that the Scripture, speaking so much of repentance and of the several duties which appertain thereunto, should ever mean, and nowhere mention, that one condition, without which all the rest is utterly of none effect? or will they say, because our Saviour hath said to his ministers, "Whose sins ye retain," etc., and because they can remit no more than what the offenders have confessed, that therefore, by the virtue of his promise, it standeth with the righteousness of God to take away no man's sins until, by auricular confession, they be opened unto the priest?

[6.] They are men that would seem to honour antiquity, and none more to depend upon the reverend judgment thereof. I dare boldly affirm, that for many hundred years after Christ, the Fathers held no such opinion; they did not gather by our Saviour's words any such necessity of seeking the priest's absolution from sin by secret and (as they now term it) sacramental confession. Public confession they thought necessary by way of discipline, not private confession, as in the nature of a sacrament, necessary.

---

[1] Annot. Rhem. in Sac. v. [2] De Pœnitentia, lib. iii. c. 4.
[3] 1 John i. 9. [C. and P.]

For, to begin with the purest times, it is unto them which read and judge without partiality a thing most clear, that the ancient ἐξομολόγησις or confession, defined by Tertullian[1] to be a discipline of humiliation and submission, framing men's behaviour in such sort as may be fittest to move pity; the confession which they used to speak of in the exercise of repentance, was made openly in the hearing of the whole, both ecclesiastical consistory and assembly.

This is the reason wherefore he perceiving that divers were better content their sores should secretly fester and eat inward, than be laid so open to the eyes of many, blameth greatly their unwise bashfulness; and, to reform the same, persuadeth with them, saying,[2] "Amongst thy brethren and fellow-servants, which are partakers with thee of one and the same nature, fear, joy, grief, sufferings, (for of one common Lord and Father we have all received one spirit,) why shouldest thou not think with thyself, that they are but thine own self? wherefore dost thou avoid them, as likely to insult over thee, whom thou knowest subject to the same haps? At that which grieveth any one part, the whole body cannot rejoice, it must needs be that the whole will labour and strive to help that wherewith a part of itself is molested."

St. Cyprian, being grieved with the dealings of them who in time of persecution had through fear betrayed their faith, and notwithstanding thought by shift to avoid in that case the necessary discipline of the Church, wrote for their better instruction the book entitled *De Lapsis*; a treatise concerning such as had openly forsaken their religion, and yet were loth openly to confess their fault in such manner as they should have done: in which book he compareth with this sort of men, certain others which had but a purpose only to have departed from the faith; and yet could not quiet their minds, till this very secret and hidden fault was confessed:[3]

---

[1] De Pœnitentia, c. 9. [C. and P.]
[2] Tertull. de Pœnit. c. 10.
[3] De Laps. c. 14.

"How much both greater in faith, (saith St. Cyprian,) and also as touching their fear better, are those men who although neither sacrifice nor libel[1] could be objected against them, yet because they thought to have done that which they should not, even this their intent they dolefully open unto God's priests? They confess that whereof their conscience accuseth them, the burden that presseth their minds they discover; they foreslow not of smaller and slighter evils to seek remedy." He saith, they declared their fault, not to one only man in private, but revealed it to God's priests; they confessed it before the whole consistory of God's ministers.

Salvianus, (for I willingly embrace their conjecture, who ascribe those homilies to him which have hitherto by common error passed under the counterfeit name of Eusebius Emisenus,)[2] I say Salvianus, though coming long after Cyprian in time, giveth nevertheless the same evidence for this truth, in a case very little different from that before alleged. His words are these, "Whereas, most dearly beloved, we see that penance oftentimes is sought and sued for by holy souls, which even from their youth have bequeathed themselves a precious treasure unto God, let us know that the inspiration of God's good Spirit moveth them so to do for the benefit of his Church, and let such as are wounded learn to inquire for that remedy, whereunto the very soundest do thus offer and obtrude as it were themselves, that if the virtuous do bewail small offences, the others cease not to lament great. And surely, when a man, that hath less need, performeth, *sub oculis Ecclesiæ*, in the view, sight, and beholding of the whole Church, an office worthy of his faith and compunction for sin, the good which others thereby reap is his own harvest, the heap of his rewards groweth by that which another gaineth, and, through a kind of spiritual usury,

---

[1] Those who had, by payment of a sum of money to the heathen magistrate, obtained exemption from sacrificing to idols, were called Libellatici, from the Libellum or certificate which they held.

[2] Hom. i. de init. Quadrages. (tom. v. par. i. p. 552. Biblioth. Patr. Lat. Col. edit. Agripp. 1618).

from that amendment of life which others learn by him, there returneth lucre into his coffers."

The same Salvianus, in another of his homilies,[1] "If faults haply be not great and grievous, (for example, if a man have offended in word, or in desire, worthy of reproof, if in the wantonness of his eye, or the vanity of his heart,) the stains of words and thoughts are by daily prayer to be cleansed, and by private compunction to be scoured out: but if any man, examining inwardly his own conscience, have committed some high and capital offence, as, if by bearing false witness he have quelled and betrayed his faith, and by rashness of perjury have violated the sacred name of truth; if with the mire of lustful uncleanness he hath sullied the veil of baptism, and the gorgeous robe of virginity; if, by being the cause of any man's death, he have been the death of the new man within himself; if, by conference with soothsayers, wizards, and charmers, he hath enthralled himself to Satan: these and such like committed crimes cannot thoroughly be taken away with ordinary, moderate, and secret satisfaction; but greater causes do require greater and sharper remedies, they need such remedies as are not only sharp, but solemn, open, and public."[2] Again, "Let that soul (saith he) answer me, which through pernicious shamefacedness is now so abashed to acknowledge his sin *in conspectu fratrum*, before his brethren, as he should have been so abashed to commit the same, what he will do in the presence of that Divine tribunal, where he is to stand arraigned in the assembly of a glorious and celestial host?"

I will hereunto add but St. Ambrose's testimony; for the places which I might allege are more than the cause itself needeth: "There are many (saith he)[3] who, fearing the judgment that is to come, and feeling inward remorse of conscience, when they have offered themselves unto penitency, and are enjoined what they

---

[1] Hom. x. ad Monach. [p. 587].
[2] "Graviores et acriores, et publicas curas requirunt."
[3] Lib. ii. de Pœnitentia, c. 9.

54   Testimony of Gennadius

Ch. iv. § 6. shall do, give back for the only scar [1] which they think that public supplication will put them unto." He speaketh of them which sought voluntarily to be penanced, and yet withdrew themselves from open confession, which they that are penitents for public crimes could not possibly have done, and therefore it cannot be said he meaneth any other than secret sinners in that place.

Gennadius, a presbyter of Marseilles, in his book touching Ecclesiastical Assertions, maketh but two kinds of confession necessary: the one in private to God alone for smaller offences; "Although (saith he) [2] a man be bitten with a conscience of sin, let his will be from thenceforward to sin no more; let him, before he communicate, satisfy with tears and prayers, and then putting his trust in the mercy of Almighty God (whose wont is to yield to godly confession) let him boldly receive the sacrament. But I speak this of such as have not burdened themselves with capital sins. Them I exhort to satisfy first by public penance, that so being reconciled by the sentence of the priest, they may communicate safely with others."

Thus still we hear of public confessions, although the crimes themselves discovered were not public; we hear that the cause of such confessions was not the openness, but the greatness, of men's offences; finally, we hear that the same, being now held by the Church of Rome to be sacramental, were the only penitential confessions used in the Church for a long time, and esteemed as necessary remedies against sin.

They which will find auricular confessions in Cyprian, therefore, must seek out some other passage than that which Bellarmine allegeth; [3] "Whereas in smaller faults which are not committed against the Lord Himself, there is a competent time assigned unto penitency, and that confession is made, after that observation [4] and trial had been had of the penitent's

---

[1] For the only scar: *i.e.* for fear of the shame.
[2] c. 53.
[3] Cypr. Epist. 12 (al. 17. c. 1. apud Bellarmin. de Pœnit. i. 3. cap. 7).
[4] "Inspecta vita ejus qui agit pœnitentiam."

behaviour, neither may any communicate till the bishop and clergy have laid their hands upon him; how much more ought all things to be warily and stayedly observed, according to the discipline of the Lord, in these most grievous and extreme crimes?" St. Cyprian's speech is against rashness in admitting idolaters to the holy communion, before they had shewed sufficient repentance, considering that other offenders were forced to stay out their time, and that they made not their public confession, which was the last act of penitency, till their life and conversation had been seen into, not with the eye of auricular scrutiny, but of pastoral observation, according to that in the council of Nice, where thirteen years being set for the penitency of certain offenders, the severity of this decree is mitigated with special caution:[1] "That, in all such cases, the mind of the penitent, and the manner of his repentance, is to be noted, that as many as with fears and tears and meekness, and the exercise of good works, declared themselves to be converts indeed, and not in outward appearance only, towards them the bishop at his discretion might use more lenity." If the council of Nice suffice not, let Gratian, the founder of the canon law, expound Cyprian, who sheweth,[2] that the stint of time in penitency, is either to be abridged or enlarged, as the penitent's faith and behaviour shall give occasion. "I have easilier found out men (saith St. Ambrose)[3] able to keep themselves free from crimes, than conformable to the rules which in penitency they should observe." St. Gregory, bishop of Nyssa, complaineth and inveigheth bitterly against them, who in the time of their penitency lived even as they had done always before:[4] "Their countenance as cheerful, their attire as neat, their diet as costly, and their sleep as secure as ever, their worldly business

---

[1] Conc. Nic. par. 2. c. 12. Pro fide et conversatione pœnitentium.
[2] De Pœnit. dist. i. cap. Mensuram.
[3] Ambros. de Pœnitentia, lib. ii. cap. 10.
[4] Greg. Nyss. Orat. in eos qui alios acerbe judicant. (Tom. ii. p. 136. ed. Par. 1638.)

Ch. iv. § 7. purposely followed, to exile pensive thoughts from their minds, repentance pretended, but indeed nothing less expressed." These were the inspections of life, whereunto St.Cyprian alludeth; as for auricular examinations, he knew them not.

[7.] Were the Fathers then without use of private confession as long as public was in use? I affirm no such thing. The first and ancientest that mentioneth this confession is Origen, by whom it may seem that men, being loth to present rashly themselves and their faults unto the view of the whole Church, thought it best to unfold first their minds to some one special man of the clergy, which might either help them himself, or refer them to a higher court, if need were. "Be therefore circumspect (saith Origen)[1] in making choice of the party to whom thou meanest to confess thy sin; know thy physician before thou use him; if he find thy malady such as needeth to be made public, that others may be the better by it, and thyself sooner helped, his counsel must be obeyed." That which moved sinners thus voluntarily to detect themselves both in private and in public, was fear to receive with other Christian men the mysteries of heavenly grace, till God's appointed stewards and ministers did judge them worthy. It is in this respect that St. Ambrose findeth fault with certain men which sought imposition of penance, and were not willing to wait their time, but would be presently admitted communicants.[2] "Such people (saith he) do seek, by so rash and preposterous desires, rather to bring the priest into bonds than to loose themselves."[3] In this respect it is that St. Augustine hath likewise said,[4] "When the wound of sin is so wide, and the disease so far gone, that the medicinable body and blood of our Lord may not be touched, men are by the bishop's authority to sequester themselves from the

---

[1] Origen in Psal. xxvii.
[2] Ambros. de Pœnitentia, lib. ii. cap. 9.
[3] "Si non tam se solvere cupiunt quam sacerdotem ligare."
[4] Aug. Hom. de Pœnitentia (Serm. 351, c. 4).

Of Penance and Mutual Confession

altar, till such time as they have repented, and be after[1] reconciled by the same authority."

Furthermore, because the knowledge how to handle our own sores is no vulgar and common art, but we either carry towards ourselves, for the most part, an over-soft and gentle hand, fearful of touching too near the quick; or else, endeavouring not to be partial, we fall into timorous scrupulosities, and sometimes into those extreme discomforts of mind, from which we hardly do ever lift up our heads again; men thought it the safest way to disclose their secret faults, and to crave imposition of penance from them whom our Lord Jesus Christ hath left in his Church to be spiritual and ghostly physicians, the guides and pastors of redeemed souls, whose office doth not only consist in general persuasions unto amendment of life, but also in private particular cure of diseased minds.

Howsoever the Novatianists presume to plead against the Church (saith Salvianus)[2] that "every man ought to be his own penitentiary, and that it is a part of our duty to exercise, but not of the Church's authority to impose or prescribe, repentance"; the truth is otherwise, the best and strongest of us may need, in such cases, direction:[3] "What doth the Church in giving penance, but shew the remedies which sin requireth? or what do we in receiving the same, but fulfil her precepts? what else but sue unto God with tears and fasts, that his merciful ears may be opened?" St. Augustine's exhortation is directly to the same purpose:[4] "Let every man whilst he hath time judge himself, and change his life of his own accord; and when this is resolved, let him, from the disposers of the holy sacraments,[5] learn in what manner he is to pacify God's displeasure." But the greatest thing which made men forward and willing, upon their knees, to confess what-

---

[1] After: *i.e.* afterwards.
[2] Hom. de Pœnitentia Niniv. (tom. v. par. i. p. 569).
[3] *Ibid.*
[4] Aug. Hom. de Pœnit. (i. Serm. 351. c. 4. § 9) citatur a Grat. dist. 1. cap. *judicet.*
[5] "A præpositis sacramentorum accipiat satisfactionis suæ modum."

soever they had committed against God, and in no wise to be withheld from the same with any fear of disgrace, contempt or obloquy, which might ensue, was their fervent desire to be helped and assisted with the prayers of God's saints. Wherein, as St. James doth exhort unto mutual confession,[1] alleging this only for a reason, that just men's devout prayers are of great avail with God: so it hath been heretofore the use of penitents for that intent to unburden their minds, even to private persons, and to crave their prayers. Whereunto Cassianus alluding, counselleth:[2] "That if men possessed with dulness of spirit be themselves unapt to do that which is required, they should in meek affection seek health at the least by good and virtuous men's prayers unto God for them." And to the same effect Gregory, bishop of Nyssa:[3] "Humble thyself, and take unto thee such of thy brethren as are of one mind, and do bear kind affection towards thee, that they may together mourn and labour for thy deliverance. Shew me thy bitter and abundant tears, that I may blend my own with them."

But because of all men there is or should be none in that respect more fit for troubled and distressed minds to repair unto, than God's ministers, he proceedeth further:[4] "Make the priest, as a father, partaker of thy affliction and grief; be bold to impart unto him the things that are most secret, he will have care both of thy safety and of thy credit."

"Confession (saith Leo)[5] is first to be offered to God, and then to the priest, as to one which maketh supplication for the sins of penitent offenders." Suppose we, that men would ever have been easily drawn, much less of their own accord have come, unto public confession, whereby they knew they should sound the trumpet of their own disgrace; would they willingly have done

---

[1] Jas. v. 16.
[2] Cassian. col. 20. c. 8.
[3] Greg. Nyss. oratione in eos qui alios acerbe judicant (*ad fin.* p. 137)
[4] *Ibid.*
[5] Leo, Ep. 80 ad Episcop. Campan. etc., citat. a Grat. de Pœnit. d. 1. c. *sufficit.*

this, which naturally all men are loth to do, but for the singular trust and confidence which they had in the public prayers of God's Church? "Let thy mother, the Church, weep for thee (saith Ambrose),[1] let her wash and bathe thy faults with her tears: our Lord doth love that many should become supplicant for one." In like sort, long before him, Tertullian:[2] "Some few assembled make a Church, and the Church is as Christ himself; when thou dost therefore put forth thy hands to the knees of thy brethren, thou touchest Christ, it is Christ unto whom thou art a supplicant: so when they pour out tears over them, it is even Christ that taketh compassion; Christ which prayeth when they pray: neither can that easily be denied, for which the Son is himself contented to become a suitor."

[8.] Whereas in these considerations, therefore, voluntary penitents had been long accustomed, for great and grievous crimes, though secret, yet openly both to repent and confess as the canons of ancient discipline required; the Greek Church first, and in process of time the Latin, altered this order, judging it sufficient and more convenient, that such offenders should do penance and make confession in private only. The cause why the Latins did, Leo declareth, saying,[3] "Although that ripeness of faith be commendable, which for the fear of God doth not fear to incur shame before all men; yet because every one's crimes are not such, that it can be free and safe for them to make publication of all things wherein repentance is necessary; let a custom, so unfit to be kept, be abrogated, lest many forbear to use remedies of penitency, whilst they either blush or are afraid to acquaint their enemies with those acts, for which the laws may take hold upon them. Besides, it shall win the more to repentance, if the consciences of sinners be not emptied into the people's ears." And to this only cause doth Sozomen[4] impute the change which the Grecians made, by ordaining throughout all churches

---

[1] Ambr. lib. ii. de Pœnit. c. 10.
[2] Tertull. de Pœnit. (c. 10).
[3] Leo, Ep. 80.
[4] E. H. vii. 16. (C. and P.)

certain penitentiaries[1] to take the confessions, and appoint the penances of secret offenders. Socrates[2] (for this also may be true, that more inducements than one did set forward an alteration so generally made) affirmeth the Grecians (and not unlikely) to have specially respected therein the occasion, which the Novatianists took at the multitude of public penitents, to insult over the discipline of the Church, against which they still cried out wheresoever they had time and place, "He that sheweth sinners favour, doth but teach the innocent to sin": and therefore they themselves admitted no man to their communion upon any repentance which once was known to have offended after baptism, making sinners thereby not the fewer, but the closer and the more obdurate, how fair soever their pretence might seem.

[9.] The Grecians' canon, for some one presbyter in every Church to undertake the charge of penitency, and to receive their voluntary confessions which had sinned after baptism, continued in force for the space of above one hundred years,[3] till Nectarius, and the bishops of churches under him, began a second alteration, abolishing even that confession which their penitentiaries took in private. There came to the penitentiary of the Church of Constantinople a certain gentlewoman, and to him she made particular confession of her faults committed after baptism, whom thereupon he advised to continue in fasting and prayer, that as with tongue she had acknowledged her sins, so there might appear likewise in her some work worthy of repentance: but the gentlewoman goeth forward, and detecteth herself of a crime, whereby they were forced to disrobe an ecclesiastical person, that is, to degrade a deacon of the same Church. When the matter by this mean came to public notice, the people were in a kind of tumult

---

[1] Penitentiaries: *i.e.* confessors.

[2] Probably Nicephorus, referring to Socrates (lib. xii. cap. 28). (C. and P.)

[3] From the schism of Novatian, circ. 253, to the episcopate of Nectarius, circ. 391. (C. and P.)

offended, not only at that which was done, but much more, because the Church should thereby endure open infamy and scorn. The clergy was perplexed and altogether doubtful what way to take, till one Eudæmon, born in Alexandria, but at that time a priest in the Church of Constantinople, considering that the cause of voluntary confession, whether public or private, was especially to seek the Church's aid, as hath been before declared, lest men should either not communicate with others, or wittingly hazard their souls if so be they did communicate, and that the inconvenience which grew to the whole Church was otherwise exceeding great, but especially grievous by means of so manifold offensive detections, which must needs be continually more, as the world did itself wax continually worse, (for antiquity, together with the gravity and severity thereof, saith Sozomen, had already begun by little and little to degenerate into loose and careless living, whereas before offences were less, partly through bashfulness in them which open their own faults, and partly by means of their great austerity which sate as judges in this business,) these things Eudæmon having weighed with himself, resolved[1] easily the mind of Nectarius, that the penitentiaries' office must be taken away, and for participation in God's holy mysteries every man be left to his own conscience; which was, as he thought, the only means to free the Church from danger of obloquy and disgrace. "Thus much (saith Socrates)[2] I am the bolder to relate, because I received it from Eudæmon's own mouth, to whom mine answer was at that time, Whether your counsel, sir, have been for the Church's good, or otherwise; God knoweth. But I see you have given occasion, whereby we shall not now any more reprehend one another's faults, nor observe that apostolic precept which saith, Have no fellowship with the unfruitful works of darkness, but rather be ye also re-

---

[1] Resolved: *i.e.* persuaded: "caused" (as we should say) "Nectarius to come to the resolution," etc.

[2] Socr. Hist. Eccles. lib. v. c. 19 *fin.*

provers of them." With Socrates, Sozomen both agreeth in the occasion of abolishing penitentiaries; and, moreover, testifieth also,[1] that in his time, living with the younger Theodosius, the same abolition did still continue, and that the bishops had in a manner every where followed the example given them by Nectarius.

[10.] Wherefore, to implead the truth of this history, Cardinal Baronius allegeth that Socrates, Sozomen, and Eudæmon were all Novatianists; and that they falsify[2] in saying, (for so they report,) that as many as held the consubstantial being of Christ, gave their assent to the abrogation of the fore-rehearsed canon. The sum is, he would have it taken for a fable, and the world to be persuaded that Nectarius did never any such thing.[3] Why then should Socrates first, and afterwards Sozomen, publish it? To please their pew-fellows, the disciples of Novatian? A poor gratification, and they very silly friends that would take lies for good turns. For the more acceptable the matter was, being deemed true, the less they must needs (when they found the contrary) either credit, or affect[4] him which had de-

---

[1] Sozom. Hist. Eccles. lib. vii. c. 16.

[2] Falsify : *i.e.* tell lies. Cf. Bishop South, Sermons : " This point have we gained, that it is absolutely and universally unlawful to lie and *falsify*."

[3] " Tanta hæc Socrati testanti præstanda est fides, quanta cæteris hæreticis de suis dogmatibus tractantibus ; quippe Novatianus secta cum fuerit, quam vere ac sincere hæc scripserit adversus pœnitentiam in Ecclesia administrari solitam, quemlibet credo posse facile judicare." Baron. vol. i. An. Chr. 56. [c. 26].

"Sozomenum eandem prorsus causam fovisse certum est. Nec Eudæmonem illum alium quam Novatianæ sectæ hominem fuisse credendum est." *Ibidem.*

" Sacerdos ille merito a Nectario est gradu amotus officioque depositus, quo facto Novatiani (ut mos est hæreticorum) quamcunque licet levem, ut sinceris dogmatibus detrahant, accipere ausi occasionem, non tantum presbyterum pœnitentiarium in ordinem redactum, sed et pœnitentiam ipsam una cum eo fuisse proscriptam, calumniose admodum conclamarunt, cum tamen illa potius theatralis fieri interdum solita peccatorum fuerit abrogata." *Ibidem* [c. 33].

[4] Affect : *i.e.* be fond of. Cf. White's Selborne, letter v. : " There are few quails, because they more *affect* open lands than enclosures." Cf. 'affection.'

-ceived them. Notwithstanding, we know that joy and gladness, rising from false information, do not only make men so forward to believe that which they first hear, but also apt to scholy[1] upon it, and to report as true whatsoever they wish were true. But so far is Socrates from any such purpose, that the fact[2] of Nectarius, which others did both like and follow, he doth disallow and reprove. His speech to Eudæmon, before set down, is proof sufficient that he writeth nothing but what was famously[3] known to all, and what himself did wish had been otherwise. As for Sozomen's correspondency with heretics, having shewed to what end the Church did first ordain penitentiaries, he addeth immediately, that Novatianists, which had no care of repentance, could have no need of this office. Are these the words of a friend or enemy? Besides, in the entrance of that whole narration, "Not to sin (saith he)[4] at all, would require a nature more divine than ours is: but God hath commanded to pardon sinners; yea, although they transgress and offend often." Could there be any thing spoken more directly opposite to the doctrine of Novatian?

Eudæmon was presbyter under Nectarius. To Novatianists the emperor gave liberty of using their religion quietly by themselves, under a bishop of their own, even within the city, for that they stood with the Church in defence of the Catholic faith against all other heretics besides. Had therefore Eudæmon favoured their heresy, their camps were not pitched so far off but he might at all times have found easy access unto them. Is there any man that hath lived with him, and hath touched him that way? if not, why suspect we him more than Nectarius?

Their report, touching Grecian Catholic bishops, who gave approbation to that which was done, and did also the like themselves in their own churches, we have no

---

[1] Scholy: *i.e.* enlarge. Cf. Hooker, in another book of the Polity, "The preacher should want a text whereupon to *scholy*."
[2] Fact: *i.e.* action; Latin, factum.
[3] Famously: *i.e.* notoriously.
[4] Lib. vii. c. 16.

reason to discredit without some manifest and clear evidence brought against it. For of Catholic bishops, no likelihood but that their greatest respect to Nectarius, a man honoured in those parts no less than the bishop of Rome himself in the western churches, brought them both easily and speedily unto conformity with him; Arians, Eunomians, Apollinarians, and the rest that stood divided from the Church, held their penitentiaries as before. Novatianists from the beginning had never any, because their opinion touching penitency was against the practice of the Church therein, and a cause why they severed themselves from the Church: so that the very state of things, as they then stood, giveth great show of probability to his speech, who hath affirmed,[1] "That they only which held the Son consubstantial with the Father, and Novatianists which joined with them in the same opinion, had no penitentiaries in their churches, the rest retained them." By this it appeareth, therefore, how Baronius, finding the relation plain, that Nectarius did abolish even those private secret confessions which the people had been before accustomed to make to him that was penitentiary, laboureth what he may to discredit the authors of the report, and leave it imprinted in men's minds, that whereas Nectarius did but abrogate public confession, Novatianists have maliciously forged the abolition of private; as if the odds between these two were so great in the balance of their judgment, which equally hated or contemned both; or, as if it were not more clear than light, that the first alteration which established penitentiaries, took away the burden of public confession in that kind of penitents; and therefore, the second must either abrogate private, or nothing.

[11.] Cardinal Bellarmine, therefore, finding that against the writers of the history it is but in vain to stand upon so doubtful terms and exceptions, endeavoureth mightily to prove, even by their report, no other confession taken away than public, which penitentiaries

---

[1] Socrates, Hist. Eccles. lib. v. c. 19.

Of Penitency and Confession

used in private to impose upon public offenders: "For why? It is (saith he)[1] very certain, that the name of penitents in the Fathers' writings signifieth only public penitents; certain, that to hear the confessions of the rest was more than one could possibly have done; certain, that Sozomen, to shew how the Latin Church retained in his time what the Greek had clean cast off, declareth the whole order of public penitency used in the Church of Rome, but of private he maketh no mention." And, in these considerations, Bellarmine will have it the meaning of both Socrates and Sozomen, that the former episcopal constitution, which first did erect penitentiaries, could not concern any other offenders than such as publicly had sinned after baptism; that only they were prohibited to come to the holy communion, except they did first in secret confess all their sins to the penitentiary, by his appointment openly acknowledge their open crimes, and do public penance for them; that whereas, before Novatian's uprising, no man was constrainable to confess publicly any sin, this canon enforced public offenders thereunto, till such time as Nectarius thought good to extinguish the practice thereof.

Let us examine, therefore, these subtle and fine conjectures, whether they be able to hold the touch. "It seemeth good" (saith Socrates) "to put down the office of these priests which had charge of penitency." What charge that was, the kinds of penitency then usual must make manifest.[2] There is often speech in the Fathers' writings, in their books frequent mention of penitency, exercised within the chambers of our heart, and seen of God, and not communicated to any other, the whole charge of which penitency is imposed of God, and doth rest upon the sinner himself. But if penitents in secret, being guilty of crimes whereby they knew they had made themselves unfit guests for the table of our Lord, did seek direction for their better performance of that

---

[1] Bellarmin. de Pœnitentia, lib. iii. c. 14.
[2] Τοὺς ὑπὸ τῆς μετανοίας περι- ελεῖν πρεσβυτέρους. [Hist. Eccles. lib. v. c. 19.]

Ch. iv. § 11. which should set them clear, it was in this case the penitentiary's office to take their confessions, to advise them the best way he could for their souls' good, to admonish them, to counsel them, but not to lay upon them more than private penance. As for notorious wicked persons, whose crimes were known, to convict, judge, and punish them was the office of the ecclesiastical consistory; penitentiaries had their institution to another end. But unless we imagine that the ancient time knew no other repentance than public, or that they had little occasion to speak of any other repentance, or else that in speaking thereof they used continually some other name, and not the name of repentance, whereby to express private penitency, how standeth it with reason, that whensoever they write of penitents, it should be thought they meant only public penitents? The truth is, they handle all three kinds,[1] but private and voluntary repentance much oftener, as being of far more general use; whereas public was but incident unto few, and not oftener than once incident unto any. Howbeit, because they do not distinguish one kind of penitency from another by difference of names, our safest way for construction is to follow circumstance of matter, which in this narration will not yield itself appliable[2] only unto public penance, do what they can that would so expound it.

They boldly and confidently affirm, that no man being compellable to confess publicly any sin before Novatian's time, the end of instituting penitentiaries afterwards in the Church was, that by them men might be constrained unto public confession. Is there any record in the world which doth testify this to be true? There is that testifieth the plain contrary: for Sozomen, declaring purposely the cause of their institution, saith,[3] "That whereas men openly craving pardon at God's

---

[1] All three kinds: *i.e.* where confession is,
(i.) privately made to God.
(ii.) privately made to the confessor.
(iii.) publicly made to the Church.

[2] Appliable: *i.e.* applicable.

[3] Sozomen, Hist. Eccl. lib. vii. c. 16.

hands, (for public confession, the last act of penitency, was always made in the form of a contrite prayer unto God,) it could not be avoided, but they must withal confess what their offences were." This, in the opinion of their prelate, seemed from the first beginning (as we may probably think) to be somewhat burdensome; that men, whose crimes were unknown, should blaze their own faults, as it were, on the stage, acquainting all the people with whatsover they had done amiss. And, therefore, to remedy this inconvenience, they laid the charge upon one only priest, chosen out of such as were of best conversation, a silent and a discreet man, to whom they which had offended might resort, and lay open their lives. He, according to the quality of every one's transgressions, appointed what they should do or suffer, and left them to execute it upon themselves. Can we wish a more direct and evident testimony, that the office here spoken of was to ease voluntary penitents from the burden of public confessions, and not to constrain notorious offenders thereunto? That such offenders were not compellable to open confessions till Novatian's time, that is to say, till after the days of persecution under Decius the emperor, they of all men should not so peremptorily avouch; with whom, if Fabian, bishop of Rome, who suffered martyrdom in the first year of Decius, be of any authority and credit, it must enforce them to reverse their sentence; his words are so plain and clear against them.[1] "For such as commit those crimes, whereof the Apostle hath said, They that do them shall never inherit the kingdom of heaven, must (saith he) be forced unto amendment, because they slip down into hell, if ecclesiastical authority stay them not." Their conceit[2] of impossibility, that one man should suffice to take the general charge of penitency in such a church as Constantinople, hath risen from a mere erroneous supposal, that the ancient manner of private confession was like the shrift at this

---

[1] Fab. Decret. Ep. 2. tom. i. Conc. p. 358.   [2] Conceit: *i.e.* conception.

68 The Course of ancient Penitential Discipline

day usual in the Church of Rome, which tieth all men at one certain time to make confession; whereas confession was then neither looked for, till men did offer it, nor offered for the most part by any other than such as were guilty of heinous transgressions, nor to them any time appointed for that purpose. Finally, the drift which Sozomen had in relating the discipline of Rome, and the form of public penitency there retained even till his time, is not to signify that only public confession was abrogated by Nectarius, but that the West or Latin Church held still one and the same order from the very beginning, and had not, as the Greek, first cut off public voluntary confession by ordaining, and then private by removing penitentiaries.

Wherefore, to conclude, it standeth, I hope, very plain and clear, first, against the one cardinal,[1] that Nectarius did truly abrogate confession in such sort as the ecclesiastical history 'hath reported; and secondly, as clear against them both,[2] that it was not public confession only which Nectarius did abolish.

[12.] The paradox in maintenance whereof Hessels[3] wrote purposely a book touching this argument, to shew that Nectarius did but put the penitentiary from his office, and not take away the office itself,[4] is repugnant to the whole advice which Eudæmon gave, of leaving the people from that time forward to their own consciences; repugnant to the conference between Socrates and Eudæmon, wherein complaint is made of some inconvenience which the want of the office would breed; finally, repugnant to that which the history declareth concerning other churches, which did as Nectarius had done

---

[1] *i.e.* Baronius; see ante.
[2] *i.e.* Baronius and Bellarmine.
[3] Theological professor at Louvain; present at the Council of Trent, where he died 1551. Fleury, Hist. Eccl. lib. 147. c. 104. (C. and P.)
[4] "Nec est quod sibi blandiantur illi de facto Nectarii, cum id potius secretorum peccatorum confessionem comprobet, et non aliud quam presbyterum pœnitentialem illo officio suo moverit; uti amplissime deducit D. Johannes Hasselus." Pamel. in Cypr. lib. de annot. 98, et in lib. Tertull. de Pœnit. annot. 1 (p. 200, Paris, 1598).

The Course did not imply Auricular Confession 69

before them, not in deposing the same man, (for that was impossible,) but in removing the same office out of their churches, which Nectarius had banished from his. For which cause, Bellarmine doth well reject the opinion of Hessels, howsoever it please Pamelius to admire it as a wonderful happy invention. But in sum, they are all gravelled, no one of them able to go smoothly away, and to satisfy either others or himself, with his own conceit concerning Nectarius.

[13.] Only in this they are stiff, that auricular confession Nectarius did not abrogate, lest if so much should be acknowledged, it might enforce them to grant that the Greek Church at that time held not confession, as the Latin now doth, to be the part of a sacrament instituted by our Saviour Jesus Christ, which therefore the Church till the world's end hath no power to alter. Yet seeing that as long as public voluntary confession of private crimes did continue in either church, (as in the one it remaineth not much above two hundred years, in the other about four hundred,) the only acts of such repentance were, first, the offender's intimation of those crimes to some one presbyter, for which imposition of penance was sought; secondly, the undertaking of penance imposed by the bishop; thirdly, after the same performed and ended, open confession to God in the hearing of the whole Church; whereupon, fourthly, ensued the prayer of the Church; fifthly, then the bishop's imposition of hands; and so, sixthly, the party's reconciliation or restitution to his former right in the holy sacrament: I would gladly know of them which make only private confession a part of their sacrament of penance, how it could be so in those times. For where the sacrament of penance is ministered, they hold that confession to be sacramental which he receiveth who must absolve; whereas during the fore-rehearsed manner of penance, it can nowhere be shewed, that the priest to whom secret information was given did reconcile or absolve any; for how could he, when public confession was to go before reconciliation, and reconciliation likewise in public thereupon to ensue? So that if they did account any confession sacramental, it was surely public, which is now abolished in the Church of Rome; and as for that which the Church of Rome doth so esteem, the ancients neither had it in such estimation, nor thought it to be of so absolute necessity for the taking away of sin.

But (for any thing that I could ever observe out of them) although not only in crimes open and notorious, which made men unworthy and incapable of holy mysteries, their discipline required first public penance, and then granted that which St. Jerome mentioneth, saying,[1] "The priest layeth his hand upon the penitent, and by invocation entreateth that the Holy Ghost may return to him again; and so, after having enjoined solemnly all the people to pray for him, reconcileth to the altar him who was delivered to Satan for the destruction of his flesh, that his spirit might be safe in the day of the Lord."—Although, I say, not only in such offences being famously[2] known to the world, but also, if the same were committed secretly, it was the custom of those times, both that private intimation should be given and public confession made thereof; in which respect whereas all men did willingly the one, but would as willingly have withdrawn themselves from the other had they known how; "Is it tolerable (saith St. Ambrose)[3] that to sue to God thou shouldst be ashamed, which blushest not to seek and sue unto man? should it grieve thee to be a suppliant to him from whom thou canst not possibly hide thyself; when to open thy sins to him, from whom, if thou wouldest, thou mightest conceal them, it doth not any thing at all trouble thee? This thou art loth to to do in the Church, where, all being sinners, nothing is more opprobrious indeed than concealment of sin, the most humble the best thought of, and the lowliest ac-

---

[1] "Sacerdos imponit manum subjecto, reditum Spiritus Sancti invocat, atque ita eum, qui traditus fuerat Satanæ in interitum carnis, ut Spiritus salvus fieret, indicta in populum oratione, altari reconciliat." Hier. advers. Lucif. [§ 5. col. 291. vol. iv.]

[2] Famously: *i.e.* publicly.

[3] Ambros. de Pœnit. lib. ii. c. 10.

counted the justest." All this notwithstanding, we should do them very great wrong to father any such opinion upon them, as if they did teach it a thing impossible for any sinner to reconcile himself unto God without confession unto the priest.

Would Chrysostom,[1] thus persuaded, have said, "Let the inquiry and punishment of thy offences be made in thine own thoughts; let the tribunal whereat thou arraignest thyself be witness; let God, and only God, see thee and thy confession"?

Would Cassianus, so believing, have given counsel[2] "That if any were withheld by bashfulness from discovering their faults to men, they should be so much the more instant and constant in opening them by supplication to God himself, whose wont is to help without publication of men's shame, and not to upbraid them when he pardoneth"?

Finally, would Prosper, settled in this opinion, have made it, as touching reconciliation to God, a matter indifferent,[3] "Whether men of ecclesiastical order did detect their crimes by confession, or leaving the world ignorant thereof, would separate voluntarily themselves for a time from the altar, though not in affection, yet in execution of their ministry, and so bewail their corrupt life"? Would he have willed them, as he doth, "to made bold of it, that the favour of God being either way recovered by fruits of forcible repentance, they should not only receive whatsoever they had lost by sin, but also, after this their new enfranchisement, aspire to endless joys of that supernal city"? To conclude, we everywhere find the use of confession, especially public, allowed of and commended by the Fathers; but that extreme and rigorous necessity of auricular and private confession, which is at this day so mightily upheld by the Church of Rome, we

---

[1] Chrys. Hom. Περὶ μετανοίας καὶ ἐξομολογήσεως. Παρὰ τοῖς λογισμοῖς γενέσθω τῶν πεπλημμελημένων ἡ ἐξέτασις, ἀμάρτυρον ἔστω τὸ δικαστήριον· ὁ Θεὸς ὁράτω μόνος ἐξομολογούμενον.

[2] Cassian. collat. 20, c. 8.

[3] Prosper de Vita Contemp. lib. ii. c. 7.

find not. It was not then the faith and doctrine of God's Church, as of the papacy at this present;—1. That the only remedy for sin after baptism is sacramental penitency. 2. That confession in secret is an essential part thereof. 3. That God himself cannot now forgive sin without the priest. 4. That, because forgiveness at the hands of the priest must arise from confession in the offenders, therefore to confess unto him is a matter of such necessity, as being not either in deed, or, at the least, in desire performed, excludeth utterly from all pardon, and must consequently in Scripture be commanded wheresoever any promise of forgiveness is made. No, no; these opinions have youth in their countenance, antiquity knew them not, it never thought nor dreamed of them.

[14.] But to let pass the papacy. Forasmuch as repentance doth import [1] alteration within the mind of a sinful man, whereby, through the power of God's most gracious and blessed Spirit, he seeth, and with unfeigned sorrow acknowledgeth, former offences committed against God, hath them in utter detestation, seeking pardon for them in such sort as a Christian should do, and with a resolute purpose settleth himself to avoid them, leading, as near as God shall assist him, for ever after, an unspotted life; and in the order (which Christian religion hath taught for procurement of God's mercy towards sinners) confession is acknowledged a principal duty, yea, in some cases, confession to man, not to God only: it is not in reformed churches denied by the learneder sort of divines,[2] but that even this confession, cleared from all errors, is both lawful and behoveful for God's people.

Confession by man being either private or public, private confession to the minister alone touching secret crimes, or absolution thereupon ensuing, as the one, so the other is neither practised by the French discipline, nor used in any of those churches which have been cast by the French mould. Open confession to be made in the face of the whole congregation by notorious malefactors, they hold necessary; howbeit not necessary

---

[1] Import: *i.e.* imply.　　　[2] Calv. Instit. lib. iii. c. iv. § 7.

Judgment of Foreign Churches on Confession 73

towards the remission of sins,[1] but only in some sort to content the Church, and that one man's repentance may seem to strengthen many, which before have been weakened by one man's fall.

Saxonians and Bohemians in their discipline constrain no man to open confession. Their doctrine is,[2] that whose faults have been public, and thereby scandalous unto the world, such, when God giveth them the spirit of repentance, ought as solemnly to return, as they have openly gone astray: first, for the better testimony of their own unfeigned conversion unto God; secondly, the more to notify their reconcilement unto the Church; and lastly, that others may make benefit of their example.

But concerning confession in private, the churches of Germany, as well the rest as Lutherans, agree, that all men should at certain times confess their offences to God in the hearing of God's ministers, thereby to shew how their sins displease them; to receive instruction for the warier carriage of themselves hereafter; to be soundly resolved, if any scruple or snare of conscience do entangle their minds; and, which is most material, to the end that men may at God's hand seek every one his own particular pardon, through the power of those keys, which the minister of God using according to our blessed Saviour's institution, in that case it is their part to accept the benefit thereof as God's most merciful ordinance for their good, and, without any distrust or doubt, to embrace joyfully his grace so given them according to the word of our Lord, which hath said,[3] "Whose sins ye remit they are remitted." So that grounding upon this assured belief, they are to rest with minds encouraged and persuaded concerning the forgiveness of all their

---

[1] "Sed tantum ut Ecclesiæ sit aliqua ratione satisfactum, et omnes unius pœnitentia confirmentur, qui fuerant unius peccatis et scandalis vulnerati." Sadeel. in Psal. xxxii. ver. 5. [Antoine la Roche de Chandieu, a leading French Protestant teacher, first at Paris, then at Geneva, 1534-1591. He Hebraized his name — Sadeel, "Chant de Dieu."] [C. and P.] See Appendix, 'Sadeel.'

[2] Harm. Conf. sect. viii. ex. 5 cap. Conf. Bohem.

[3] John xx. 23. Cap. 5, Confess. Bohem.

sins, as out of Christ's own word and power by the ministry of the keys.

[15.] It standeth with us in the Church of England, as touching public confession, thus:

First, seeing day by day we in our Church begin our public prayers to Almighty God with public acknowledgment of our sins, in which confession every man, prostrate as it were before his glorious Majesty, crieth against himself, and the minister with one sentence pronounceth universally all clear whose acknowledgment so made hath proceeded from a true penitent mind; what reason is there every man should not, under the general terms of confession, represent to himself his own particulars whatsoever, and adjoining thereunto that affection which a contrite spirit worketh, embrace to as full effect the words of divine grace, as if the same were severally and particularly uttered with addition of prayers, imposition of hands, or all the ceremonies and solemnities that might be used for the strengthening of men's affiance in God's peculiar mercy towards them? Such complements are helps to support our weakness, and not causes that serve to procure or produce his gifts. If with us there be "truth in the inward parts," as David speaketh, the difference of general and particular forms in confession and absolution is not so material that any man's safety or ghostly good should depend upon it.

And for private confession and absolution it standeth thus with us:

[1] The minister's power to absolve is publicly taught and professed, the Church not denied to have authority either of abridging or enlarging the use and exercise of that power, upon the people no such necessity imposed of opening their transgression unto men, as if remission of sins otherwise were impossible; neither any such opinion had of the thing itself, as though it were either unlawful or unprofitable, save only for these inconveniences which the world hath by experience observed in it heretofore. And in regard thereof, the Church of

---

[1] "As for private confession, abuses and errors set apart, we condemn it not, but leave it at liberty." Jewel, Defen. par. 156.

Of Private Confession and Absolution in our Church 75

England hath hitherto thought it the safer way to refer men's hidden crimes unto God and themselves only; howbeit, not without special caution for the admonition of such as come to the holy Sacrament, and for the comfort of such as are ready to depart the world. First, because there are but few that consider how much that part of divine service which consists in partaking the holy Eucharist, doth import their souls; what they lose by neglect thereof, and what by devout practice they might attain unto: therefore, lest carelessness of general confession should, as commonly it doth, extinguish all remorse of men's particular enormous crimes, our custom (whensoever men present themselves at the Lord's table) is, solemnly to give them very fearful admonition, what woes are perpendicularly hanging over the heads of such as dare adventure to put forth their unworthy hands to those admirable mysteries of life, which have by rare examples been proved conduits of irremediable death to impenitent receivers; whom therefore, as we repel being known, so being not known, we cannot but terrify. Yet, with us, the ministers of God's most holy word and sacraments, being all put in trust with the custody and dispensation of those mysteries, wherein our communion is, and hath been ever, accounted the highest grace that men on earth are admitted unto, have therefore all equally the same power to withhold that sacred mystical food from notorious evil-livers, from such as have any way wronged their neighbours, and from parties between whom there doth open hatred and malice appear, till the first sort have reformed their wicked lives, the second recompensed them unto whom they were injurious, and the last condescended unto some course of Christian reconciliation, whereupon their mutual accord may ensue. In which cases, for the first branch of wicked life and the last, which is open enmity, there can arise no great difficulty about the exercise of his power; in the second, concerning wrongs, there[1] may, if men shall presume to define or measure injuries according to their own conceits, depraved oftentimes as well

---

[1] I have altered the word 'they,' which is in the original text, to 'there,' as being almost necessary to the construction of the passage.

76 Temporary Excommunication by the Minister

by error as partiality, and that no less in the minister himself, than in any other of the people under him.[1]

The knowledge, therefore, which he taketh of wrongs must rise, as it doth in the other two, not from his own opinion or conscience, but from the evidence of the fact which is committed; yea, from such evidence as neither doth admit denial nor defence. For if the offender, having either colour of law to uphold, or any other pretence to excuse, his own uncharitable and wrongful dealings, shall wilfully stand in defence thereof, it serveth as a bar to the power of the minister in this kind.[2] Because (as it is observed by men of very good judgment in these affairs) "although in this sort our separating of them be not to strike them with the mortal wound of excommunication, but to stay them rather from running desperately headlong into their own harm; yet it is not in us to sever from the holy communion but such as are either found culpable by their own confession, or have been convicted in some public secular or ecclesiastical court. For who is he that dares take upon him to be any man's both accuser and judge?"[3] "Evil persons are not rashly, and as we list, to be thrust from communion with the Church. Insomuch that, if we cannot proceed against them by any orderly course of judgment, they rather are to be suffered for the time than molested. Many there are reclaimed, as Peter; many, as Judas,

---

[1] I have, in this sentence, mainly adopted the reading of the text which will be found in C. and P.—The original reading is highly laboured and involved.

[2] "Nos a communione quenquam prohibere non possumus, quamvis hæc prohibitio nondum sit mortalis, sed medicinalis, nisi aut sponte confessum, aut aliquo sive seculari sive ecclesiastico judicio accusatum atque convictum. Quis enim sibi utrumque audet assumere, ut cuiquam ipse sit et accusator et judex?" [Rhenan. admon. de dogm. Tertull. inter opp. Tertull. p. 903 ed. Par. 1635.]

[3] "Non enim temere et quodammodo libet, sed propter judicium, ab Ecclesiæ communione separandi sunt mali, ut si propter judicium auferri non possint, tolerentur potius, velut paleæ cum tritico. Multi corriguntur, ut Petrus; multi tolerantur, ut Judas; multi nesciuntur, donec veniat Dominus, et illuminabit abscondita tenebrarum." [Rhenan. admonit. de dogmat. Tertull. *Ibid.*]

Of a Death-bed Repentance

known well enough, and yet tolerated; many which must remain undescried till the day of his appearance, by whom the secret corners of darkness shall be brought into open light."

Leaving therefore unto his judgment them whom we cannot stay from casting their own souls into so great hazard, we have, in the other part of penitential jurisdiction in our power and authority to release sin, joy on all sides, without trouble or molestation unto any. And if to give be a thing more blessed than to receive, are we not infinitely happier in being authorized to bestow the treasure of God, than when necessity doth constrain to withdraw the same?

They which, during life and health, are never destitute of ways to delude [1] repentance, do notwithstanding oftentimes, when their last hour draweth on, both feel that sting which before lay dead in them, and also thirst after such helps as have been always, till then, unsavoury. St. Ambrose's words touching late repentance are somewhat hard:[2] "If a man be penitent and receive absolution, (which cannot in that case be denied him,) even at the very point of death, and so depart, I dare not affirm he goeth out of the world well; I will not counsel man to trust to this, because I am loth to deceive any man, seeing I know not what to think of it. Shall I judge such a one a castaway? Neither will I avouch him safe: all I am able to say, is, let his estate be left to the will and pleasure of Almighty God. Wilt thou be therefore delivered of all doubt? Repent while yet thou art healthy and strong. If thou defer it till time give no longer possibility of sinning, thou canst not be thought to have left sin, but rather sin to have forsaken thee." Such admonitions may in their time and place be necessary, but in no wise prejudicial to the generality of God's heavenly promise, "Whensoever a sinner doth repent from the bottom of his heart, I will put out all his iniquity." And of this, although it hath pleased God not to leave to the world any multitude of exam-

---

[1] Perhaps the better reading would be "elude."
[2] Lib. iii. de Pœnit.

ples, lest the careless should too far presume, yet one He hath given, and that most memorable, to withhold from despair in the mercies of God, at what instant soever man's unfeigned conversion be wrought.[1] Yea, because to countervail the fault of delay, there are in the latest repentance oftentimes the surest tokens of sincere dealing; therefore upon special confession made to the minister of God, he presently absolveth in this case the sick party from all sins by that authority which Jesus Christ hath committed unto him, knowing that God respecteth not so much what time is spent, as what truth is shewed in repentance.

[16.] In sum, when the offence doth stand only between God and man's conscience, the counsel is good which St. Chrysostom giveth:[2] "I wish thee not to bewray thyself publicly, nor to accuse thyself before others. I wish thee to obey the Prophet, who saith, Disclose thy way unto the Lord, confess thy sins before him; tell thy sins to him that he may blot them out. If thou be abashed to tell unto any other wherein thou hast offended, rehearse them every day between thee and thy soul. I wish thee not to confess them to thy fellow-servant, who may upbraid thee with them; tell them to God, who will cure them: there is no need for thee in the presence of witnesses to acknowledge them; let God alone see thee at thy confession. I pray and beseech you, that you would more often than you do

---

[1] St. Luke xxiii. 42, 43.

[2] "Non dico tibi, ut te prodas in publicum, neque ut te apud alios accuses, sed obedire te volo Prophetæ dicenti, 'revela Domino viam tuam.' Ante Deum confitere peccata tua; peccata tua dicito, ut ea deleat; si confunderis alicui dicere quæ peccasti, dicito ea quotidie in anima. Non dico ut confitearis conservo qui exprobret; Deo dicito qui ea curat; non necesse est præsentibus testibus confiteri; solus te Deus confitentem videat. Rogo et oro ut crebrius Deo immortali confiteamini, et enumeratis vestris delictis, veniam petatis. Non te in theatrum conservorum duco, non hominibus peccata tua conor detegere. Repete coram Deo conscientiam tuam, te explica, ostende medico præstantissimo vulnera tua, et pete ab eo medicamentum." Chrysost. Hom. 31 ad Hebr. et in Psal. 59, Hom. de pœn. et confess. et Hom. 5 de incarn. Dei natura, Homil. itemque de Lazaro.

confess to God eternal, and, reckoning up your trespasses, desire his pardon. I carry you not into a theatre or open court of many of your fellow-servants, I seek not to detect your crimes before men; disclose your conscience before God, unfold yourselves to him, lay forth your wounds before him, the best physician that is, and desire of him salve for them." If hereupon it follow, as it did with David, "I thought, I will confess against myself my wickedness unto thee, O Lord, and thou forgavest me the plague of my sin," we have our desire, and there remaineth only thankfulness accompanied with perpetuity of care to avoid that, which, being not avoided, we know we cannot remedy without new perplexity and grief. Contrariwise, if peace with God do not follow the pains we have taken in seeking after it, if we continue disquieted and not delivered from anguish, mistrusting whether that we do be sufficient; it argueth that our sore doth exceed the power of our own skill, and that the wisdom of the pastor must bind up those parts, which being bruised are not able to be recured of themselves.

CHAPTER V.

OF SATISFACTION.

[1.] There resteth now Satisfaction only to be considered, a point which the Fathers do often touch, albeit they never aspire to such mysteries as the papacy hath found enwrapped within the folds and plaits thereof. And it is happy for the Church of God that we have the writings of the Fathers to shew what their meaning was. The name of Satisfaction, as the ancient Fathers mean it, containeth whatsoever a penitent should do in the humbling himself unto God, and testifying by deeds of contrition the same which confession in words pretendeth; "He which by repentance for sins (saith Tertullian,[1] speaking of fickle-minded men) had a purpose to satisfy the Lord, will now by repenting his repentance make Satan satisfaction; and be so much the more hateful to God, as he is unto God's enemy

[1] Tertull. de Pœnit. (c. 5).

more acceptable." Is it not plain, that satisfaction doth here include the whole work of penitency, and that God is satisfied when we are restored through sin into favour by repentance? "How canst thou (saith Chrysostom)[1] move God to pity thee, when thou wilt not seem as much as to know that thou hast offended?" By appeasing, pacifying, and moving God to pity, St. Chrysostom meaneth the very same with the Latin Fathers, when they speak of satisfying God. "We feel (saith Cyprian)[2] the bitter smart of his rod and scourge, because there is in us neither care to please him with our good deeds, nor to satisfy him for our evil." Again,[3] "Let the eyes which have looked on idols, sponge out their unlawful acts with those sorrowful tears, which have power to satisfy God." The Master of Sentences[4] allegeth out of St. Augustine that which is plain enough to this purpose: [5] "Three things there are in perfect penitency, compunction, confession, and satisfaction; that as we three ways offend God, namely, in heart, word, and deed, so by three duties we may satisfy God."

Satisfaction, as a part, comprehendeth only that which the papists meant by *worthy of repentance*; and if we speak of the whole work of repentance itself, we may, in the phrase of antiquity, term it very well satisfaction.

[2.] Satisfaction is a work which justice requireth to be done for contentment of persons injured: neither is it in the eye of justice a sufficient satisfaction, unless it fully equal the injury for which we satisfy. Seeing then that sin against God eternal and infinite must needs be an infinite wrong; justice, in regard thereof, doth necessarily exact an infinite recompense, or else inflict upon the offender infinite punishment. Now, because God was thus to be satisfied, and man not able to make satisfaction in such sort, his unspeakable love and inclination to save mankind from eternal death, ordained in our behalf a Mediator to do that which had been for

---

[1] Chrysost. in 1 Cor. Hom. 8. Τὸν Θεὸν ἐξιλεώσασθαι.
[2] Cypr. Ep. 8 [al. 11. c. 2].
[3] Ep. 26 [al. 31. c. 5].
[4] *i.e.* Peter Lombard: see Appendix. The references in the notes are to the commentaries of Bonaventure on his 'Sentences.'
[5] Bonav. in Sent. lib. iv. dis. 16.

any other impossible. Wherefore all sin is remitted in the only faith of Christ's passion,[1] and no man without belief thereof justified. Faith alone maketh Christ's satisfaction ours; howbeit, that faith alone, which after sin maketh us by conversion his.

For inasmuch as God will have the benefit of Christ's satisfaction both thankfully acknowledged, and duly esteemed of all such as enjoy the same, he therefore imparteth so high a treasure unto no man, whose faith hath not made him willing by repentance to do even that, which of itself how unavailable soever, yet being required and accepted with God, we are in Christ thereby made capable and fit vessels to receive the fruits of his satisfaction: yea, we so far please and content God, that because when we have offended he looketh but for repentance at our hands; our repentance and the works thereof are therefore termed satisfactory, not for that so much is thereby done as the justice of God can exact, but because such actions of grief and humility in man after sin are *illices divinæ misericordiæ*, (as Tertullian speaketh of them,)[2] they draw that pity of God towards us, wherein he is for Christ's sake contented, upon our submission, to pardon our rebellion against him; and when that little which his law appointeth is faithfully executed, it pleaseth him in tender compassion and mercy to require no more.

[3.] Repentance is a name which noteth the habit and operation of a certain grace or virtue in us: Satisfaction, the effect which it hath, either with God or man. And it is not in this respect said amiss, that satisfaction importeth acceptation, reconciliation, and amity; because that, through satisfaction on the one part made, and allowed on the other, they which before did reject are now content to receive, they to be won again which were lost, and they to love unto whom just cause of hatred was given. We satisfy therefore, in doing that which is sufficient to this effect; and they towards whom we do it are satisfied, if they accept it as suffi-

---

[1] Bonav. in Sent. lib. iv. dis. xv. q. 9.   [2] De Pœn. c. 9.

cient, and require no more: otherwise we satisfy not, although we do satisfy.[1] For so between man and man it oftentimes falleth out, but between man and God never. It is therefore true, that our Lord Jesus Christ by one most precious and propitiatory sacrifice, which was his body, a gift of infinite worth, offered for the sins of the whole world, hath thereby once reconciled us to God, purchased his general free pardon, and turned divine indignation from mankind. But we are not for that cause to think any office of penitence either needless or fruitless on our own behalf: for then would not God require any such duties at our hands. Christ doth remain everlastingly a gracious intercessor, even for every particular penitent. Let this assure us that God, how highly soever displeased and incensed with our sins, is notwithstanding, for his sake, by our tears, pacified, taking that for satisfaction which is done by us, because Christ hath by his satisfaction made it acceptable. For, as he is the high-priest of our salvation, so he hath made us priests likewise[2] under Him, to the end we might offer unto God praise and thankfulness while we continue in the way of life; and when we sin, the satisfactory or propitiatory sacrifice of a broken and contrite heart. There is not any thing that we do that could pacify God and clear us in his sight from sin, if the goodness and mercy of our Lord Jesus Christ were not;[3] whereas now, beholding the poor offer of our religious endeavours meekly to submit ourselves as often as we have offended, he regardeth with infinite mercy those services which are as nothing, and with words of comfort reviveth our afflicted minds, saying, "It is I, even I, that taketh away thine iniquities for mine own sake." Thus doth repentance satisfy God, changing his wrath and indignation into mercy.

[4.] Anger and mercy are in us passions; but in him not so. "God (saith St. Basil)[4] is no ways passionate;

---

[1] *i.e.* what we do may be called, technically, a satisfaction, but it is not sufficient.
[2] Rev. i. 6.
[3] Cassian. col. 20. c. 8.
[4] Basil. Hom. in Psalm 37. Παντὸς γὰρ πάθους ἀλλότριον τὸ Θεῖον.

but because the punishments which his judgment doth inflict are, like effects of indignation, severe and grievous to such as suffer them, therefore we term the revenge which he taketh upon sinners, anger; and the withdrawing of his plagues, mercy." "His wrath (saith St. Augustine)[1] is not as ours, the trouble of a mind disturbed and disquieted with things amiss, but a calm, unpassionate, and just assignation of dreadful punishment to be their portion which have disobeyed; his mercy a free determination of all felicity and happiness unto men, except their sins remain as a bar betwixt it and them." So that when God doth cease to be angry with sinful men, when he receiveth them into favour, when he pardoneth their offences, and remembereth their iniquities no more, (for all these signify but one thing,) it must needs follow, that all punishments before due in revenge of sin, whether they be temporal or eternal, are remitted.

For how should God's indignation import only man's punishment, and yet some punishment remain unto them towards whom there is now in God no indignation remaining? "God (saith Tertullian)[2] takes penitency at men's hands; and men at his, in lieu thereof, receive impunity"; which notwithstanding doth not prejudice the chastisements which God, after pardon, hath laid upon some offenders, as on the people of Israel,[3] on Moses,[4] on Miriam,[5] on David,[6] either for their own[7] more sound amendment, or for[8] example

---

[1] "Cum Deus irascitur, non ejus significatur perturbatio qualis est in animo irascentis hominis; sed, ex humanis moribus translato vocabulo, vindicta ejus, quæ non nisi justa est, iræ nomen accepit." Aug. Ench. cap. 33.

[2] "Pœnitentiæ compensatione redimendam proponit impunitatem Deus." Tertull. de Pœnit. (c. 6).

[3] Num. xiv. 22.

[4] Num. xx. 12.

[5] Num. xii. 14.

[6] 2 Sam. xii. 14.

[7] "Cui Deus vere propitius est, non solum condonat peccata ne noceant ad futurum seculum, sed etiam castigat, ne semper peccare delectet." Aug. in Psal. xcviii. (§ 11).

[8] "Plectuntur quidam, quo cæteri corrigantur; exempla sunt omnium, tormenta paucorum." Cypr. de Lapsis [c. 13].

unto others in this present world, (for in the world to come punishments have unto these intents no use, the dead being not in case to be better by correction, nor to take warning by executions of God's justice there seen;) but assuredly to whomsoever he remitteth sin, their very pardon is in itself a full, absolute, and perfect discharge for revengeful punishment, which God doth now here threaten, but, with purpose of revocation if men repent, nowhere inflict but on them whom impenitency maketh obdurate.

Of the one therefore it is said,[1] "Though I tell the wicked, Thou shalt die the death, yet if he turneth from his sin, and do that which is lawful and right, he shall surely live and not die." Of the other,[2] "Thou, according to thine hardness, and heart that will not repent, treasurest up to thyself wrath against the day of wrath, and evident appearance of the judgment of God." If God be satisfied and do pardon sin, our justification restored is as perfect as it was at the first bestowed. For so the Prophet Isaiah witnesseth,[3] "Though your sins were as crimson, they shall be made as white as snow; though they were as scarlet, they shall be as white as wool." And can we doubt concerning the punishment of revenge, which was due to sin, but that if God be satisfied and have forgotten his wrath, it must be, even as St. Augustine reasoneth, [4] "What God hath covered he will not observe, and what he observeth not he will not punish." The truth of which doctrine is not to be shifted off by restraining it unto eternal punishment alone. For then would not David have said,[5] "They are blessed to whom God imputeth not sin"; blessedness having no part or fellowship at all with malediction. Whereas to be subject to revenge for sin, although the punishment be but temporal, is to be under the curse of the law: wherefore, as one and the same fire consumeth stubble

---

[1] Ezek. xxxiii. 14.
[2] Rom. ii. 5.
[3] Isaiah i. 18.
[4] "Si texit Deus peccata, noluit advertere; si noluit advertere, noluit animadvertere." August.
[5] Ps. xxxii. 2.

and refineth gold, so if it please God to lay punishment
on them whose sins he hath forgiven; yet is not this
done for any destructive end of wasting and eating
them out, as in plagues inflicted upon the impenitent,
neither is the punishment of the one as of the other
proportioned by the greatness of sin past, but according
to that future purpose whereunto the goodness of God
referreth it, and wherein there is nothing meant to the
sufferer but furtherance of all happiness, now in grace,
and hereafter in glory. St. Augustine, to stop the
mouths of Pelagians arguing, "That if God had imposed death upon Adam, and Adam's posterity, as a
punishment of sin, death should have ceased when God
procured sinners their pardon"; answereth, first,[1] "It is
no marvel, either that bodily death should not have
happened to the first man, unless he had first sinned,
(death as punishment following his sin,) or that after
sin is forgiven, death notwithstanding befalleth the
faithful; to the end that the strength of righteousness
might be exercised by overcoming the fear thereof."
So that justly God did inflict bodily death on man for
committing sin, and yet after sin forgiven took it not
away, that his righteousness might still have whereby
to be exercised. He fortifieth this with David's
example, whose sin he forgave, and yet afflicted him for
exercise and trial of his humility. Briefly, a general
axiom he hath for all such chastisements, "Before forgiveness, they are the punishment of sinners; and after
forgiveness, they are exercises and trials of righteous
men."[2] Which kind of proceeding is so agreeable with
God's nature and man's comfort, that it seemeth even

---

[1] "Mirandum non est, et mortem corporis non fuisse eventuram homini, nisi præcessisset peccatum, cujus etiam talis pœna consequeretur, et post remissionem peccatorum eam fidelibus evenire, ut ejus timorem vincendo exerceretur fortitudo justitiæ. Sic et mortem corporis propter hoc peccatum Deus homini inflixit, et post peccatorum remissionem propter exercendam justitiam non ademit." Aug. de pecc. mer. et rem. lib. ii. c. 34.

[2] "Ante remissionem esse illa supplicia peccatorum, post remissionem autem certamina, exercitationesque justorum." August. *Ibid.*; Cypr. Epist. 53.

injurious to both, if we should admit those surmised reservations of temporal wrath in God appeased towards reconciled sinners.[1] As a Father he delights in his children's conversion, neither doth he threaten the penitent with wrath, or them with punishment which already mourn; but by promise assureth such of indulgence and mercy, yea, even of plenary pardon, which taketh away all both faults and penalties: there being no reason why we should think him the less just because he sheweth himself thus merciful; when they, which before were obstinate, labour to appease his wrath with the pensive meditation of contrition, the meek humility which confession expresseth, and the deeds wherewith repentance declareth itself to be an amendment as well of the rotten fruit, as the dried leaves and withered root of the tree. For with these duties by us performed, and presented unto God in heaven by Jesus Christ, whose blood is a continual sacrifice of propitiation for us, we content, please, and satisfy God.

[5.] Repentance therefore, even the sole virtue of repentance, without either purpose of shrift, or desire of absolution from the priest; repentance, the secret conversion of the heart, in that it consisteth of these three,[2] and doth by these three pacify God, may be without hyperbolical terms most truly magnified, as a recovery of the soul of man from deadly sickness, a restitution of glorious light to his darkened mind, a comfortable reconciliation with God, a spiritual nativity, a rising from the dead, a day-spring from the depth of obscurity, a redemption from more than Egyptian thraldom, a grinding of the old Adam even into dust and powder, a deliverance out of the prisons of hell, a

---

[1] *i.e.* the chastisements being for men's good, to withdraw them, because God was appeased, would only be to injure forgiven sinners. The sentence, as it stands in the text, is somewhat involved.

[2] *i.e.* Contrition, Confession, and Satisfaction. See chap. iii. sect. 5 ante; and Hooker's remarks which follow.

full restoration of the seat of grace and throne of glory, a triumph over sin, and a saving victory.

[6.] Amongst the works of satisfaction, the most respected have been always these three, Prayers, Fasts, and Alms-deeds: by prayer, we lift up our souls to him from whom sin and iniquity have withdrawn them; by fasting, we reduce the body from thraldom under vain delights, and make it serviceable for parts of virtuous conversation; by alms, we dedicate to charity those worldly goods and possessions, which unrighteousness doth neither get nor bestow well: the first, a token of piety intended towards God; the second, a pledge of moderation and sobriety in the carriage of our own persons; the last, a testimony of our meaning to do good to all men. In which three, the Apostle, by way of abridgment, comprehendeth whatsoever may appertain to sanctimony,[1] holiness, and good life:[2] as contrariwise, the very mass of general corruption throughout the world, what is it but only forgetfulness of God, carnal pleasure, immoderate desire after worldly things, profaneness, licentiousness, covetousness? All offices to repentance have these two properties; there is in performance of them painfulness, and in their nature a contrariety unto sin. The one consideration causeth them both in holy Scripture[3] and elsewhere to be termed judgment or revenges taken voluntarily on ourselves, and to be furthermore also preservatives from future evils, inasmuch as we commonly use to keep with the greater care, that which with pain we have recovered.[4] And they are in the other respect contrary to sin committed: contrition, contrary to the pleasure; confession, to the error, which is the mother of sin; and to the deeds of sin, the works of satisfaction contrary: therefore they are the more effectual to cure the evil habit thereof. Hereunto it was that St. Cyprian re-

---

[1] Sanctimony: *i.e.* sanctified conduct.
[2] The reference is perhaps to Acts x. 2 and 30.
[3] 2 Cor. vii. 11.

[4] Ἡμῶν γὰρ αὐτῶν δίκην λάβωμεν, ἡμῶν αὐτῶν κατηγορήσωμεν· οὕτως ἐξιλεωσόμεθα τὸν κριτήν. Chrys. Hom. 30, in Ep. ad Heb.

ferred his earnest and vehement exhortation,[1] "That they which had fallen, should be instant in prayer, reject bodily ornaments when once they had stripped themselves out of Christ's attire, abhor all food after Satan's morsels tasted, follow works of righteousness which wash away sin, and be plentiful in alms-deeds wherewith souls are delivered from death." Not as if God did, according to the manner of corrupt judges, take some money to abate so much in the punishment of malefactors. "These duties must be offered (saith Salvianus)[2] not in confidence to redeem or buy out sin, but as tokens of meek submission; neither are they with God accepted, because of their value, but for our affection's sake which doth thereby shew itself." Wherefore, concerning satisfaction made to God by Christ only; and of the manner how repentance generally, particularly also, how certain special works of penitency, both are by the Fathers, in their ordinary phrase of speech, called satisfactory, and may be by us very well so acknowledged, enough hath been spoken.

[7.] Our offences sometimes are of such nature as requireth that particular men be satisfied, or else repentance to be utterly void and of none effect. For if, either through open rapine, or crooked fraud; if through injurious, or unconscionable dealing, a man have wittingly wronged others to enrich himself; the first thing evermore in this case required (ability serving) is restitution. For let no man deceive himself, from such offences we are not discharged, neither can be, till recompense and restitution to man accompany the penitent confession we have made to Almighty God. In which case, the law of Moses was direct and plain:[3] "If any sin and commit a trespass against the Lord, and deny unto his neighbour that which was given him to keep, or that which was put unto him of trust; or doth by robbery or by violence oppress his neighbour; or hath found that which was lost, and denieth it, and swears falsely: for

---

[1] Cypr. de Lapsis. c. ult. (p. 367, tom. v. par. iii. Biblioth.
[2] Salv. ad Eccl. Cath. lib. i. Patr. Lat.). [3] Lev. vi. 2, etc.

any of these things that a man doth wherein he sinneth, he that doth thus offend and trespass, shall restore the robbery that he hath taken, or the thing he hath got by violence, or that which was delivered him to keep, or the lost thing which he found ; and for whatsoever he hath sworn falsely, adding perjury to injury, he shall both restore the whole sum, and shall add thereunto a fifth part more, and deliver it unto him, unto whom it belongeth, the same day wherein he offereth for his trespass." Now, because men are commonly over-slack to perform this duty, and do therefore defer it sometime, till God hath taken the party wronged out of the world ; the law providing that trespassers might not under such pretence gain the restitution which they ought to make, appointeth the kindred surviving to receive what the dead should, if they had continued. " But (saith Moses)[1] if the party wronged have no kinsman to whom this damage may be restored, it shall then be rendered to the Lord himself for the priests' use." The whole order of proceeding herein is in sundry traditional writings set down by their great interpreters and scribes, which taught them that a trespass between a man and his neighbour can never be forgiven till the offender have by restitution made recompense for the wrongs done, yea, they hold it necessary that he appease the party grieved by submitting himself unto him ; or, if that will not serve, by using the help and mediation of others: " In this case (say they) for any man to shew himself unappeasable and cruel, were a sin most grievous, considering that the people of God should be easy to relent, as Joseph was towards his brethren ": finally, if so it fall out, that the death of him that was injured prevent his submission which did offend, let him then (for so they determine that he ought) go, accompanied with ten others, unto the sepulchre of the dead, and there make confession of the fault, saying, "I have sinned against the Lord God of Israel, and against this man, to whom I have done such or such injury ; and if money be due, let it be restored to his heirs, or in case he have none

[1] Num. v. 8.

known, leave it with the house of judgment ": that is to say, with the senators, ancients, and guides of Israel. We hold not Christian people tied unto Jewish orders for the manner of restitution ; but, surely, restitution we must hold necessary, as well in our own repentance as theirs, for sins of wilful oppression and wrong.[1]

[8.] Now, although it suffices, that the offices wherewith we pacify God or private men be secretly done ; yet in cases where the Church must be also satisfied, it was not to this end and purpose unnecessary, that the ancient discipline did further require outward signs of contrition to be shewed, confession of sin to be made openly, and those works to be apparent which served as testimonies for conversion before men. Wherein, if either hypocrisy did at any time delude their judgment,[2] they knew that God is he whom masks and mockeries cannot blind, that he which seeth men's hearts would judge them according unto his own evidence, and, as Lord, correct the sentence of his servants concerning matters beyond their reach: or, if such as ought to have kept the rules of canonical satisfaction would by sinister means and practices undermine the same, obtruding presumptuously themselves to the participation of Christ's most sacred mysteries before they were orderly re-admitted thereunto, the Church for contempt of holy things held them incapable of that grace, which God in the sacrament doth impart to devout communicants ; and no doubt but he himself did retain bound, whom the Church in those cases refused to loose.

The Fathers, as may appear by sundry decrees and canons of the primitive Church, were (in matter especially of public scandal) provident that too much facility of pardoning might not be shewed. " He that casteth off his lawful wife (saith St. Basil)[3] and doth take another, is adjudged an adulterer by the verdict of our

---

[1] " Quamdiu enim res, propter quam peccatum est, non redditur, si reddi potest, non agitur pœnitentia, sed fingitur." Sent. 4. d. 15.

[2] Cypr. Ep. lii. (al. 55. c. 10).

[3] Basil. Ep. ad. Amphil. c. 26.

Lord himself; and by our fathers it is canonically ordained, that such for the space of a year shall mourn, for two years' space hear, three years be prostrate, the seventh year assemble with the faithful in prayer, and after that be admitted to communicate, if with tears they bewail their fault."

Of them which had fallen from their faith in the time of the emperor Licinius, and were not thereunto forced by any extreme usage, the Nicene synod under Constantine ordained,[1] "That earnestly repenting, they should continue three years hearers, seven years be prostrate, and two years communicate with the people in prayer, before they came to receive the oblation." Which rigour sometimes they tempered nevertheless with lenity, the self-same synod having likewise defined, "That, whatsoever the cause were, any man desirous at the time of departure out of this life to receive the Eucharist, might (with examination and trial) have it granted him by the bishop.[2] Yea, besides this case of special commiseration, there is a canon more large, which giveth always liberty to abridge, or extend out the time, as the party's meek or sturdy disposition should require.

By means of which discipline the Church having power to hold them many years in suspense, there was bred in the minds of the penitents, through long and daily practice of submission, a contrary habit unto that which before had been their ruin, and for ever afterwards wariness not to fall into those snares out of which they knew they could not easily wind themselves. Notwithstanding, because there was likewise hope and possibility of shortening the time, this made them in all the parts and offices of their repentance the more fervent. In the first station, while they only beheld others passing towards the temple of God, whereunto for themselves to approach it was not lawful, they stood as miserable for-

---

[1] Concil. Nicen. can. 11.
[2] Καθόλου καὶ περὶ παντὸς οὑτινοσοῦν ἐξοδεύοντος αἰτοῦντος μετέχειν Εὐχαριστίας ὁ ἐπίσκοπος μετὰ δοκιμασίας μεταδιδότω τῆς προσφορᾶς, can. 13. μετὰ δοκιμασίας, id est, *manifestis indiciis deprehensa peccatoris seria conversione ad Deum*, can. 12.

Ch. v. § 8. lorn men, the very patterns of perplexity and woe. In the second, when they had the favour to wait at the doors of God, where the sound of his comfortable word might be heard, none received it with attention like to theirs. Thirdly, being taken and admitted to the next degree of prostrates at the feet, yet behind the back of that angel representing God, whom the rest saw face to face, their tears and entreaties both of pastor and people, were such as no man could resist. After the fourth step, which gave them liberty to hear and pray with the rest of the people, being so near the haven, no diligence was then slackened which might hasten admission to the heavenly table of Christ, their last desire. It is not therefore a thing to be marvelled at, though St. Cyprian took it in very ill part, when both backsliders from the faith and sacred religion of Christ laboured by sinister practice to procure from imprisoned saints those requests for present absolution, which the Church could neither yield unto with safety of discipline, nor in honour of martyrdom easily deny. For, what would thereby ensue they needed not to conjecture, when they saw how every man which came so commended to the Church by letters thought that now he needed not to crave, but might challenge of duty, his peace; taking the matter very highly, if but any little forbearance or small delay was used.[1] "He which is overthrown (saith Cyprian) menaceth them that stand, the wounded them that were never touched; and because presently he hath not the body of our Lord in his foul imbrued hands, nor the blood within his polluted lips, the miscreant fumeth at God's priests: such is thy madness, O thou furious man, thou art angry with him which laboureth to turn away God's anger from thee; him thou threatenest, which sueth unto God for grace and mercy on thy behalf."[2]

Touching Martyrs he answereth,[3] "That it ought not in this case to seem offensive, though they were denied,

---

[1] De Laps. c. 12. "Jacens stantibus, et integris vulneratus, minatur."
[2] Exod. xii. 31; Jer. vii. 15.
[3] De Laps. c. 12.

All Absolution void without previous Repentance 93

seeing God himself did refuse to yield to the piety of his own righteous saints, making suit for obdurate Jews."[1]

As for the parties, in whose behalf such shifts were used; to have their desire was, in very truth, the way to make them the more guilty: such peace granted contrary to the rigour of the Gospel, contrary to the law of our Lord and God, doth but under colour of merciful relaxation, deceive sinners, and by soft handling destroy them, a grace dangerous for the giver, and to him which receiveth it nothing at all valuable. The patient expectation that bringeth health is, by this means, not regarded; recovery of soundness not sought for by the only medicine available, which is satisfaction; penitency thrown out of men's hearts; the remembrance of that heaviest and last judgment clean banished; the wounds of dying men, which should be healed, are covered.; the stroke of death, which hath gone as deep as any bowels are to receive it, is overcast with the slight show of a cloudy look. From the altar of Satan to the holy table of the Lord, men are not afraid to come, even belching, in a manner, the sacrificed morsels they have eaten; yea, their jaws yet breathing out the irksome savour of their former contagious wickedness, they seize upon the blessed body of our Lord, nothing terrified with that dreadful commination, which saith,[2] "Whosoever eateth and drinketh unworthily, is guilty of the body and blood of Christ." They vainly think it to be peace, which is gotten before they be purged of their faults, before their crime be solemnly confessed, before their conscience be cleared by the sacrifice and imposition of the priests' hands, and before they have pacified the indignation of God. Why term they that a favour, which is an injury? Wherefore cloak they impiety with the name of charitable indulgence? Such facility giveth not, but rather taketh away, peace; and is itself another fresh persecution or trial, whereby that fraudulent enemy maketh a secret havoc of such as before he had overthrown; and now, to the end that he

[1] Ezek. xiv. 14. [2] 1 Cor. xi. 27.

may clean swallow them, he casteth sorrow into a dead sleep, putteth grief to silence, wipeth away the memory of faults newly done, smothereth the sighs that should rise from a contrite spirit, drieth up eyes which ought to send forth rivers of tears, and permitteth not God to be pacified with full repentance, whom heinous and enormous crimes have displeased.

By this then we see, that in St. Cyprian's judgment, all absolutions are void, frustrate, and of no effect, without sufficient repentance first shewed; whereas contrariwise, if true and full satisfaction have gone before, the sentence of man here given is ratified of God in heaven, according to our Saviour's own sacred testimony,[1] "Whose sins ye remit, they are remitted."

[9.] By what works in the Virtue, and by what in the Discipline, of Repentance, we are said to satisfy either God or men, cannot now be thought obscure. As for the inventors of sacramental satisfaction, they have both altered the natural order heretofore kept in the Church, by bringing in a strange preposterous course to absolve before satisfaction be made, and moreover by this their misordered practice, are grown [2] into sundry errors concerning the end whereunto it is referred.

They imagine, beyond all conceit of antiquity, that when God doth remit sin and the punishment eternal thereunto belonging, he reserveth the torments of hell-fire to be nevertheless endured for a time, either shorter or longer, according to the quality of men's crimes. Yet so, that there is between God and man a certain composition (as it were) or contract, by virtue whereof works assigned by the priests to be done after absolution shall satisfy God, as touching the punishment which he otherwise would inflict for sin pardoned and forgiven.

Now, because they cannot assure any man, that if he performeth what the priest appointeth it shall suffice; this (I say) because they cannot do, insomuch as the priest hath no power to determine or define of equi-

[1] St. John xx. 23.
[2] Are grown: *i.e.* "the inventors of sacramental satisfaction" have grown.

valency between sins and satisfactions; and yet if a penitent depart this life, the debt of satisfaction being either in whole or in part undischarged, they stedfastly hold that the soul must remain in unspeakable torment till all be paid: therefore, for help and mitigation in this case, they advise men to set certain copesmates on work, whose prayers and sacrifices may satisfy God for such souls as depart in debt. Hence have arisen the infinite pensions of their priests, the building of so many altars and tombs, the enriching of so many churches with so many glorious and costly gifts, the bequeathing of lands and ample possessions to religious companies, even with utter forgetfulness of friends, parents, wife, and children, all natural affection giving place unto that desire which men, doubtful of their own estate, have to deliver their souls from torment after death.

Yet, behold, even this being done, how far forth it shall avail they are not sure; and therefore the last upshot unto their former inventions is, that as every action of Christ did both merit for himself, and satisfy partly for the eternal, and partly for the temporal punishment due unto men for sin, so his saints have obtained the like privilege of grace, making every good work they do, not only meritorious in their own behalf, but satisfactory too for the benefit of others. Or if, having at any time grievously sinned, they do more to satisfy God than he in justice can expect or look for at their hands; the surplusage runneth to a common stock, out of which treasury containing whatsoever Christ did by way of satisfaction for temporal punishment, together with the satisfactory force which resided in all the virtuous works of saints, and in their satisfactions whatsoever doth abound, (I say,) From hence they hold God satisfied for such arrearages as men behind in accompt discharge not by other means; and for disposition hereof, as it is their doctrine that Christ remitteth not eternal death without the priest's absolution, so without the grant of the pope they cannot but teach it alike unpossible that souls in hell should receive any temporal release of pain. The sacrament

Ch. vi. § 1. of pardon from him being to this effect no less necessary, than the priest's absolution to the other. So that by this postern-gate cometh in the whole mart of papal indulgences; a gain unestimable to him, to others a spoil; a scorn both to God and man. So many works of satisfaction pretended to be done by Christ, by saints, and martyrs; so many virtuous acts possessed with satisfactory force and virtue; so many supererogations in satisfying beyond the exigence of their own necessity; and this, that the pope might make a monopoly of all, turning all to his own gain, or at least to the gain of those which are his own: such facility they have to convert a pretended sacrament into a revenue.

CHAPTER VI.
OF ABSOLUTION OF PENITENTS.

[1.] Sin is not helped but by being assecured[1] of pardon. It resteth therefore to be considered, what warrant we have concerning forgiveness, when the sentence of man absolveth us from sin committed against God. At the words of our Saviour, saying to the sick of the palsy,[2] "Son, thy sins are forgiven thee," exception was taken by the Scribes, who secretly reasoned against him,[3] "Is any able to forgive sins, but God only?" Whereupon they condemn his speech as blasphemy; the rest, which believed him to be a Prophet sent from God, saw no cause wherefore He might not as lawfully say, and as truly, to whomsoever amongst them,[4] "God hath taken away thy sins," as Nathan (they all knew) had used the very like speech; to whom David did not therefore impute blasphemy, but embraced, as became him, the words of truth with joy and reverence.

Now there is no controversion, but as God in that special case did authorize Nathan, so Christ more generally his Apostles and the ministers of his word in his name to absolve sinners. Their power being

---

[1] Assecured: *i.e.* assured.
[2] Matt. ix. 2.
[3] Mark ii. 7; Luke v. 21.
[4] 2 Sam. xii. 13.

equal, all the difference between them can be but only in this, that whereas the one had prophetical evidence, the other have the certainty partly of faith, and partly of human experience, whereupon to ground their sentence; faith, to assure them of God's most gracious pardon in heaven unto all penitents, and touching the sincerity of each particular party's repentance, as much as outward sensible tokens or signs can warrant.

[2.] It is not to be marvelled, that so great a difference appeareth between the doctrine of Rome and ours, when we teach repentance. They imply in the name of repentance much more than we do. We stand chiefly upon the due inward conversion of the heart; they more upon works of external show. We teach, above all things, that repentance which is one and the same from the beginning to the world's end; they a sacramental penance, of their own devising and shaping. We labour to instruct men in such sort, that every soul which is wounded with sin may learn the way how to cure itself; they, clean contrary, would make all sores seem incurable, unless the priests have a hand in them.

Touching the force of whose absolution they strangely hold, that whatsoever the penitent doth, his contrition, confession, and satisfaction have no place of right to stand as material parts in this sacrament, nor consequently any such force as to make them available for the taking away of sin, in that they proceed from the penitent himself without the privity of the minister, but only as they are enjoined by the minister's authority and power.[1] So that no contrition or grief of heart, till the priest exact it; no acknowledgment of sins, but that which he doth demand; no praying, no fasting, no alms, no repentance or restitution for whatsoever we have done, can help, except by him it be first imposed. It is the chain of their own doctrine, no remedy for mortal sin committed after baptism but the sacrament of penance only; no sacrament of penance, if either

---

[1] "Ipsius pœnitentis actio non est pars sacramenti, nisi quatenus potestati sacerdotali subjicitur, et a sacerdote dirigitur vel jubetur." Bellarm. de Pœnit. lib. i. cap. 16.

matter or form be wanting; no ways to make those duties a material part of the sacrament, unless we consider them as required and exacted by the priest. Our Lord and Saviour, they say, hath ordained his priests judges in such sort, that no man which sinneth after baptism can be reconciled unto God but by their sentence.[1] For why? If there were any other way of reconciliation, the very promise of Christ should be false, in saying,[2] "Whatsoever ye bind on earth, shall be bound in heaven; and whose sins soever ye retain, they are retained."[3] Except therefore the priest be willing, God hath by promise hampered himself so, that it is not now in his own power to pardon any man. Let him who hath offended crave as the publican did,[4] "Lord, be thou merciful unto me a sinner"; let him, as David, make a thousand times his supplication,[5] "Have mercy upon me, O God, according to thy loving-kindness; according to the multitude of thy compassions, put away mine iniquities"; all this doth not help, till such time as the pleasure of the priest be known, till he have signed us a pardon, and given us our *quietus est*, God himself hath no answer to make but such as that of the angel unto Lot[6]—"I can do nothing."

[3.] It is true, that our Saviour by these words, "Whose sins ye remit, they are remitted," did ordain judges over our sinful souls, gave them authority to absolve from sin, and promised to ratify in heaven whatsoever they should do on earth in execution of this their office; to the end that hereby, as well his ministers might take encouragement to do their duty with all faithfulness, as also his people admonition, gladly with all reverence to be ordered by them; both parts knowing that the functions of the one towards the other have his perpetual assistance and approbation.

---

[1] "Christus instituit sacerdotes judices super terram cum ea potestate, ut sine ipsorum sententia, nemo post baptismum lapsus reconciliari possit." Bellarmin. de Pœnit. l. iii. c. 2.

[2] Matt. xviii. 18; John x. 23.

[3] "Quod si possent ii sine sacerdotum sententia absolvi, non esset vera Christi promissio, Quæcunque," etc. Bellarm. *ibid.*

[4] Luke xviii. 13.

[5] Ps. li. 1.

[6] Gen. xix. 22.

Against Popish Absolution

Howbeit all this with two restraints, which every jurisdiction in the world hath; the one, that the practice thereof proceed in due order; the other, that it do not extend itself beyond due bounds; which bounds or limits have so confined penitential jurisdiction, that although there be given unto it power of remitting sin, yet no such sovereignty of power that no sin should be pardonable in man without it.[1] Thus to enforce our Saviour's words, is as though we should gather, that because whatsoever Joseph did command in the land of Egypt, Pharaoh's grant was, it should be done; therefore he granted that nothing should be done in the land of Egypt but what Joseph did command, and so consequently, by enabling his servant Joseph to command under him, disableth himself to command any thing without Joseph.

But by this we see how the papacy maketh all sin unpardonable, which hath not the priest's absolution; except peradventure in some extraordinary case, where albeit absolution be not had, yet it must be desired.

[4.] What is then the force of absolution? What is it which the act of absolution worketh in a sinful man? Doth it by any operation derived from itself alter the state of the soul? Doth it really take away sin, or but ascertain us[2] of God's most gracious and merciful pardon? The latter of which two is our assertion, the former theirs.

[3]At the words of our Lord and Saviour Jesus Christ,

---

[1] "Christus ordinariam suam potestatem in Apostolos transtulit; extraordinariam sibi reservavit. Ordinaria enim remedia in Ecclesia ad remittenda peccata sunt ab eo instituta, sacramenta; sine quibus peccata remittere Christus potest, sed extraordinarie et multo rarius hoc facit, quam per sacramenta. Noluit igitur eos extraordinariis remissionis peccatorum confidere, quæ et rara sunt et incerta: sed ordinaria, ut ita dicam, visibilia sacramentorum quærere remedia." Maldon. in Matt. xvi. 19.

[2] Ascertain us: *i.e.* make us sure.

[3] "The insertion of this paragraph here is probably a mistake; the whole of it, except the quotation from St. Clement, being found in other parts of this book." (C. and P.) See section 1 of this chapter, and the next paragraph.

saying unto the sick of the palsy, "Son, thy sins are forgiven thee," the Pharisees, which knew him not to be "Son of the living God," took secret exception, and fell to reasoning with themselves against him;[1] "Is any able to forgive sin but God only?" "The sins (saith St. Cyprian) that are committed against him, he alone hath power to forgive, which took upon him our sins, he which sorrowed and suffered for us, he whom the Father delivered unto death for our offences."[2] Whereunto may be added, that which Clemens Alexandrinus hath,[3] "Our Lord is profitable every way, every way beneficial, whether we respect him as man, or as God; as God forgiving, as man instructing and learning how to avoid sin. For it is 'I, even I, that putteth away thine iniquities for mine own sake, and will not remember thy sins,' saith the Lord."[4]

Now, albeit we willingly confess with St. Cyprian, "The sins which are committed against him, he only hath power to forgive, who hath taken upon him our sins, he which hath sorrowed and suffered for us, he whom God hath given for our offences";[5] yet neither did St. Cyprian intend to deny the power of the minister otherwise than if he presume beyond his commission to remit sin, where God's own will is it should be retained; for against such absolutions he speaketh, (which being granted to whom they ought to have been denied, are of no validity;) and, if rightly it be considered how higher causes in operation use to concur with inferior means, his grace with our ministry, God really performing the same which man is authorized to act as in his name, there shall need, for decision of this point, no great labour.

---

[1] Mark ii. 7; Luke v. 21.
[2] Cypr. de Lapsis, c. 11.
[3] Πάντα ὀνίνησιν ὁ Κύριος καὶ πάντα ὠφελεῖ, καὶ ὡς ἄνθρωπος, καὶ ὡς Θεός. Τὰ μὲν ἁμαρτήματα ὡς Θεὸς ἀφιείς, εἰς δὲ τὸ μὴ ἐξαμαρτάνειν παιδαγωγῶν ὡς ἄνθρωπος. Alexandr. Pædag. I i. [c.3]
[4] Isa. xliii. 25.
[5] "Veniam peccatis, quæ in ipsum commissa sunt, solus potest ille largiri, qui peccata nostra portavit, qui pro nobis doluit, quem Deus tradidit pro peccatis nostris." [De Laps. c. 11.]

Of Absolution and Remission of Sins 101

[5.] To remission of sins there are two things necessary: grace, as the only cause which taketh away iniquity; and repentance, as a duty or condition required in us. To make repentance such as it should be, what doth God demand but inward sincerity, joined with fit and convenient offices for that purpose? the one referred wholly to our own consciences, the other best discerned by them whom God hath appointed judges in this court. So that having first the promises of God for pardon generally unto all offenders penitent; and particularly for our own unfeigned meaning, the unfallible testimony of a good conscience, the sentence of God's appointed officer and vicegerent to approve with unpartial judgment the quality of that we have done, and as from his tribunal in that respect, to assoil[1] us of any crime; I see no cause but by the rules of our faith and religion we may rest ourselves very well assured touching God's most merciful pardon and grace; who, especially for the strengthening of weak, timorous, and fearful minds, hath so far endued his Church with power to absolve sinners. It pleaseth God that men sometimes should, by missing this help, perceive how much they stand bound to him for so precious a benefit enjoyed. And surely, so long as the world lived in any awe or fear of falling away from God, so dear were his ministers to the people, chiefly in this respect, that being through tyranny and persecution deprived of pastors, the doleful rehearsal of their lost felicities hath not anything more eminent, than that sinners distressed should not know how or where to unload their burdens.[2] Strange it were unto me, that the Fathers, who so much everywhere extol the grace of Jesus Christ in leaving unto his Church this heavenly and divine power, should as

---

[1] Assoil: *i.e.* absolve.

[2] The reference is to the edict of Hanneric, king of the Arian Vandals in Africa, which had driven into exile bishops, priests, deacons, and members of the Church Catholic to the number of 4,961. Part of their complaint was "Qui nobis pœnitentiæ munera collaturi sunt, et reconciliationis indulgentia abstrictos peccatorum vinculis soluturi?" [See the whole passage quoted in C. and P. from Victor. de Pers. Vand.]

Ch. vi. § 6. men, whose simplicity had universally been abused, agree all to admire and magnify a needless office.

The sentence therefore of ministerial absolution, hath two effects: touching sin, it only declareth us freed from the guiltiness thereof, and restored into God's favour; but concerning right in sacred and divine mysteries, whereof through sin we were made unworthy, as the power of the Church did before effectually bind and retain us from access unto them, so upon our apparent repentance it truly restoreth our liberty, looseth the chains wherewith we were tied, remitteth all whatsoever is past, and accepteth us no less returned than if we had never gone astray.

For, inasmuch as the power which our Saviour gave to his Church is of two kinds; the one to be exercised over voluntary penitents only, the other over such as are to be brought to amendment by ecclesiastical censures, the words wherein he hath given this authority must be so understood, as the subject or matter whereupon it worketh will permit. It doth not permit that in the former kind, (that is to say, in the use of power over voluntary converts,) to bind or loose, remit or retain, should signify any other than only to pronounce of sinners according to that which may be gathered by outward signs; because really to effect the removal or continuance of sin in the soul of any offender, is no priestly act, but a work which far exceedeth their ability. Contrariwise, in the latter kind of spiritual jurisdiction, which by censures constraineth men to amend their lives; it is true, that the minister of God doth then more declare and signify what God hath wrought. And this power, true it is, that the Church hath invested in it.

[6.] Howbeit, as other truths, so this hath by error been oppugned and depraved through abuse. The first of name that openly in writing withstood the Church's authority and power to remit sin, was Tertullian, after he had combined himself with Montanists, drawn to the liking of their heresy through the very sourness of his own nature, which neither his incredible skill and know-

The Unchaste excluded from Absolution by Tertullian 103

ledge otherwise, nor the doctrine of the Gospel itself, could but so much alter, as to make him savour any thing which carried with it the taste of lenity. A sponge steeped in wormwood and gall, a man through too much severity merciless, and neither able to endure nor to be endured of any. His book entitled *Concerning Chastity*, and written professedly against the discipline of the Church, hath many fretful and angry sentences, declaring a mind very much offended with such as would not persuade themselves, that of sins, some be pardonable by the keys of the Church, some incapable of forgiveness; that middle and moderate offences, having received chastisement, may by spiritual authority afterwards be remitted, but greater transgressions must (as touching indulgence) be left to the only pleasure of Almighty God in the world to come; that as idolatry and bloodshed, so likewise fornication and sinful lust, are of this nature; that they, which so far have fallen from God, ought to continue for ever after barred from access unto his sanctuary, condemned to perpetual profusion of tears, deprived of all expectation and hope to receive any thing at the Church's hands, but publication of their shame. "For (saith he)[1] who will fear to waste out that, which he hopeth he may recover? Who will be careful for ever to hold that, which he knoweth cannot for ever be withheld from him? He which slackeneth the bridle to sin, doth thereby give it even the spur also.[2] Take away fear, and that which presently succeedeth instead thereof is licentious desire. Greater offences therefore are punishable, but not pardonable, by the Church. If any Prophet or Apostle be found to have remitted such transgressions, they did it not by the ordinary course of discipline, but by extraordinary power. For they all raised the dead, which none but God is able to do; they restored the impotent and lame man, a work peculiar to Jesus Christ; yea, that which Christ would not do, because executions of such

---

[1] De Pudic. c. 9.   [2] "Securitas delicti, etiam libido est ejus."

severity beseemed not him who came to save and redeem the world by his sufferings, they by their power struck Elymas and Ananias, the one blind, and the other dead. Approve first yourselves to be, as they were, Apostles or Prophets, and then take upon you to pardon all men. But if the authority you have be only ministerial, and no way sovereign, over-reach not the limits which God hath set you; know that to pardon capital sin is beyond your commission."

Howbeit, as oftentimes the vices of wicked men do cause other their commendable qualities to be abhorred, so the honour of great men's virtues is easily a cloak to their errors. In which respect, Tertullian hath passed with much less obloquy and reprehension than Novatian; who, broaching afterwards the same opinion, had not otherwise wherewith to countervail the offence he gave, and to procure it the like toleration. Novatian, at the first a stoical philosopher, (which kind of men hath always accounted stupidity the highest top of wisdom and commiseration the deadliest sin,) became by institution and study the very same which the other had been before through a secret natural distemper, upon his conversion to the Christian faith and recovery from sickness, which moved him to receive the sacrament of baptism in his bed. The bishops, contrary to the canons of the Church,[1] would needs, in special love towards him, ordain him presbyter, which favour satisfied not him who thought himself worthy of greater place and dignity. He closed therefore with a number of well-minded men, and not suspicious what his secret purposes were, and having made them sure unto him by fraud, procureth his own consecration to be their bishop. His prelacy now was able, as he thought, to countenance what he intended to publish, and therefore his letters went presently abroad to sundry churches, advising them never to admit to the fellowship of holy mysteries, such as had after baptism offered sacrifice to idols.

---

[1] Concil. Neocæsar. c. 12.

Against Popish Confessions to Priests 105

There was present[1] at the council of Nice, together with other bishops, one Acesius, a Novatianist, touching whose diversity in opinion from the Church, the emperor, desirous to hear some reason, asked of him certain questions; for answer whereunto, Acesius weaveth out a long history of things that happened in the persecution under Decius, and of men which, to save life, forsook faith. But in the end was a certain bitter canon, framed in their own school: "That men which fall into deadly sin after holy baptism, ought never to be again admitted to the communion of divine mysteries; that they are to be exhorted unto repentance; howbeit not to be put in hope that pardon can be had at the priest's hands, but with God, which hath sovereign power and authority in himself to remit sin, it may be in the end they shall find mercy." These followers of Novatian, which gave themselves the title of καθαροὶ, clean, pure, and unspotted men, had one point of Montanism more than their master did profess; for amongst sins unpardonable they reckoned second marriages, of which opinion Tertullian making (as his usual manner was) a salt apology, "Such is (saith he)[2] our stony hardness, that defaming our Comforter with a kind of enormity in discipline, we dam up the doors of the Church no less against twice-married men, than against adulterers and fornicators." Of this sort therefore it was ordained by the Nicene synod, that if any such did return to the catholic and apostolic unity, they should in writing bind themselves to observe the orders of the Church, and communicate as well with them which had been often married, or had fallen in time of persecution, as with other sort of Christian people. But further to relate, or at all to refel[3] the error of misbelieving men concerning this point, is not now to our present purpose greatly necessary.

[7.] The Church may receive no small detriment by corrupt practice, even there where doctrine concerning

---

[1] Socrat. [Sozom. (?)] lib. iv. cap. 23; Concil. Nicen. c. 30.
[2] De Pudic. c. i. fin.
[3] Refel: *i.e.* refute.

Ch. vi. § 7. the substance of things practised is free from any great or dangerous corruption. If therefore that which the papacy doth in matter of confessions and absolution be offensive; if it palpably swerve in the use of the keys; howsoever that which it teacheth in general concerning the Church's power to retain and forgive sins be admitted true, have they not on the one side as much whereat to be abashed, as on the other wherein to rejoice?

They bind all men, upon pain of everlasting condemnation and death, to make confessions to their ghostly fathers of every great offence they know, and can remember, that they have committed against God. Hath Christ in his Gospel so delivered the doctrine of repentance unto the world? Did his Apostles so preach it to nations? Have the Fathers so believed or so taught? Surely Novatian was not so merciless in depriving the Church of power to absolve some certain offenders, as they in imposing upon all a necessity thus to confess. Novatian would not deny but God might remit that which the Church could not, whereas in the papacy it is maintained, that what we conceal from men, God himself shall never pardon. By which oversight as they have here surcharged the world with multitude, but much abated the weight of confessions, so the careless manner of their absolution hath made discipline, for the most part, amongst them a bare formality; yea, rather a means of emboldening unto vicious and wicked life, than either any help to prevent future, or medicine to remedy present evils in the soul of man. The Fathers were slow and always fearful to absolve any before very manifest tokens given of a true penitent and contrite spirit. It was not their custom to remit sin first, and then to impose works of satisfaction, as the fashion of Rome is now; insomuch that this their preposterous course, and misordered practices, hath bred also in them an error concerning the end and purpose of these works. For against the guiltiness of sin, and the danger of everlasting condemnation thereby incurred, confession and absolution succeeding the same, are, as they take it, a remedy sufficient; and therefore what their penitentiaries do think good to enjoin further, whether it be a number of Ave-Maries daily to be scored up, a journey of pilgrimage to be undertaken, some few dishes of ordinary diet to be exchanged, offerings to be made at the shrines of saints, or a little to be scraped off from men's superfluities for relief of poor people, all is in lieu or exchange with God, whose justice, notwithstanding our pardon, yet oweth us still some temporal punishment, either in this or in the life to come, except we quit[1] it ourselves here with works of the former kind, and continued till the balance of God's most strict severity shall find the pains we have taken equivalent with the plagues which we should endure, or else the mercy of the pope relieve us. And at this postern-gate cometh in [2] the whole mart of papal indulgences, so infinitely strewed, that the pardon of sin, which heretofore was obtained hardly and by much suit, is with them become now almost impossible to be escaped.

[8.] To set down then the force of this sentence in absolving penitents; there are in sin these three things:[3] the act which passeth away and vanisheth; the pollution wherewith it leaveth the soul defiled; and the punishment whereunto they are made subject that have committed it. The act of sin is every deed, word, and thought against the law of God:[4] "for sin is the transgression of the law"; and although the deed itself do not continue, yet is that bad quality permanent, whereby it maketh the soul unrighteous and deformed in God's sight.[5] "From the heart come evil cogitations, murders, adulteries, fornications, thefts, false testimonies, slanders; these are things which defile a man." They do not only, as effects of impurity, argue the nest to be unclean out of which they came, but as causes they strengthen that disposition unto wickedness which

---

[1] Quit: *i.e.* discharge the account. Compare the French form of receipt, "Pour acquit."
[2] See ante, c. v. sect. ix.
[3] "In peccato tria sunt; actio mala, interior macula, et sequela." Bon. sent. l. iv. d. 17. q. 3.
[4] 1 John iii. 4.
[5] Matt. xv. 19.

Ch. vi. § 8. brought them forth; they are both fruits and seeds of uncleanness, they nourish the root out of which they grow, they breed that iniquity which bred them. The blot therefore of sin abideth, though the act be transitory. And out of both ariseth a present debt, to endure what punishment soever the evil which we have done deserveth; an obligation, in the chains whereof sinners, by the justice of Almighty God, continue bound till repentance loose them. "Repent this thy wickedness, (saith Peter[1] unto Simon Magus), and beseech God, that if it be possible the thought of thine heart may be pardoned; for I see thou art in the gall of bitterness, and in the bond of iniquity." In like manner Solomon:[2] "The wicked shall be held fast in the cords of his own sin."

Nor doth God only bind sinners hand and foot by the dreadful determination of his own unsearchable judgment against them; but sometimes also the Church bindeth by the censures of her discipline.[3] So that when offenders upon their repentance are by the same discipline absolved, the Church looseth but her own bonds, the chains wherein she had tied them before.

The act of sin God alone remitteth,[4] in that his purpose is never to call it to account, or to lay it unto men's charge; the stain he washeth out by the sanctifying grace of his Spirit; and concerning the punishment of sin, as none else hath power to cast body and soul into hell-fire, so none have power to deliver either besides him.

As for the ministerial sentence of private absolution, it can be no more than a declaration what God hath done; it hath but the force of the Prophet Nathan's absolution,[5] "God hath taken away thy sin": than which construction, especially of words judicial, there is

---

[1] Acts viii. 22, 23.
[2] Prov. v. 22.
[3] "Sacerdotes opus justitiæ exercent in peccatores, cum eos justa pœna ligant; opus misericordiæ, cum de ea aliquod relaxant, vel sacramentorum communioni conciliant; alia opera in peccatores exercere nequeunt." Sent. l. iv. dis. 8.
[4] Acts vii. 60; Micah vii. 9; 1 Cor. vi. 11; Tit. iii. 5; Luke xii. 5; Matt. x. 28.
[5] 2 Sam. xii. 13.

not any thing more vulgar.¹ For example,² the publicans are said in the Gospel to have justified God ; the Jews in Malachi to have blessed proud men, which sin and prosper ; not that the one did make God righteous, or the other the wicked happy : but to bless, to justify, and to absolve, are as commonly used for words of judgment, or declaration, as of true and real efficacy ; yea, even by the opinion of the Master of Sentences.³ "It may be soundly affirmed and thought that God alone doth remit and retain sins, although he have given power to the Church to do both ; but he one way, and the Church another. He only by himself forgiveth sin, who cleanseth the soul from inward blemish, and looseth the debt of eternal death. So great a privilege he hath not given unto his priests, who notwithstanding are authorized to loose and bind, that is to say, to declare who are bound, and who are loosed. For albeit a man be already cleared before God, yet he is not in the Church of God so taken, but by the virtue of the priest's sentence; who likewise may be said to bind by imposing satisfaction, and to loose by admitting to the holy communion."

St. Jerome also, whom the Master of the Sentences allegeth for more countenance of his own opinion, doth no less plainly and directly affirm : [4] "That as the priests of the law could only discern, and neither cause nor remove, leprosies; so the ministers of the Gospel, when they retain or remit sin, do but in the one, judge how long we continue guilty, and in the other, declare when we are clear or free." For there is nothing more apparent, than that the discipline of repentance, both public and private, was ordained as an outward mean to bring men to the virtue of inward conversion ; so that when this by manifest tokens did seem effected, absolution ensuing (which could not make) served only to declare men innocent.

---

¹ Vulgar : *i.e.* common.
² Luke vii. 29 ; Mal. iii. 15.
³ *i.e.* Peter Lombard, circ. 1164. The reference is to Sent. lib. iv. dis. 18.
⁴ Hier. tom. iv. Comment. in 16 Matt.

[9.] But the cause wherefore they are so stiff, and have forsaken their own master in this point is, for that they hold the private discipline of penitency to be a sacrament; absolution an external sign in this sacrament; the signs external of all sacraments in the New Testament, to be both causes of that which they signify, and signs of that which they truly cause.

To this opinion concerning sacraments, they are now tied by expounding a canon in the Florentine council according to the former ecclesiastical invention received from Thomas.[1] For his deceit it was, that the mercy of God, which useth sacraments as instruments whereby to work, endueth them at the time of their administration with supernatural force and ability to induce grace into ths souls of men; even as the axe and saw do seem to bring timber into that fashion which the mind of the artificer intendeth. His conceit,[2] Scotus, Occam, Petrus Alliacensis, with sundry others, do most earnestly and strongly impugn, shewing very good reason wherefore no sacrament of the new law can either by virtue which itself hath, or by force supernaturally given it, be properly a cause to work grace; but sacraments are therefore said to work or confer grace, because the will of Almighty God is, although not to give them such efficacy, yet himself to be present in the ministry of the working that effect, which proceedeth wholly from him, without any real operation of theirs, such as can enter into men's souls.

[10.] In which construction, seeing that our books and writings have made it known to the world how we join with them, it seemeth very hard and injurious dealing, that Bellarmine throughout the whole course of his second book *De Sacramentis in Genere*,[3] should so boldly

---

[1] *i.e.* Thomas Aquinas.

[2] Scot. Sent. lib. iv. Solut. ad 4 quæst. et 5. Occam in lib. i. 9. 4. Alliac. quæst 1. in Sent. 4.

[3] "Lutherani in hac re interdum ita scribunt, ut videantur a catholicis non dissentire; interdum autem apertissime scribunt contraria : at semper in eadem sententia manent, sacramenta non habere immediate ullam efficientiam respectu gratiæ, sed esse nuda signa, tamen mediate

Of Sacramental Grace

face down his adversaries, as if their opinion were, that sacraments are naked, empty, and ineffectual signs; wherein there is no other force, than only such as in pictures, to stir up the mind, that so by theory and speculation of things represented, faith may grow: finally, that all the operation which sacraments have, is a sensible and divine instruction. But had it pleased him not to hoodwink his own knowledge, I nothing doubt but he fully saw how to answer himself; it being a matter very strange and incredible, that one which with so great diligence had winnowed his adversaries' writings,[1] should be ignorant of their minds. For, even as in the person of our Lord Jesus Christ, both God and man, when his human nature is by itself considered, we may not attribute that unto him, which we do and must ascribe as oft as respect is had unto both natures combined; so because in sacraments there are two things distinctly to be considered, the outward sign, and the secret concurrence of God's most blessed Spirit, in which respect our Saviour hath taught that water and the Holy Ghost are combined to work the mystery of new birth; sacraments therefore, as signs, have only those effects before mentioned; but of sacraments, in that by God's own will and ordinance they are signs assisted always with the power of the Holy Ghost, we acknowledge whatsoever either the places of Scripture, or the authority of councils and Fathers, or the proofs and arguments of reason which he allegeth, can shew to be

aliquid efficere quatenus excitant et alunt fidem — quod ipsum non faciunt nisi repræsentando, ut sacramenta per visum excitent fidem, quemadmodum prædicatio Verbi per auditum." Bellarm. de effect. Sacram. l. ii. c. 2.

"Quædam signa sunt theorica, non ad alium finem instituta, quam ad significandum; alia ad significandum et efficiendum, quæ ob id practica dici possunt. Controversia est inter nos et Hæreticos, quod illi faciunt sacramenta signa prioris generis. Quare si ostendere poterimus esse signa posterioris generis obtinuimus causam." *Ibid.* c. 8.

[1] "Semper memoria repetendum est sacramenta nihil aliud quam instrumentales esse conferandæ nobis gratiæ causas." Calv. in Ant. con. Trid. sect. 7. c. 5. "Si qui sint qui negent sacramentis contineri gratiam quam figurant, illos improbamus." *Ibid.* c. 6.

wrought by them. The elements and words have power of infallible signification, for which they are called seals of God's truth; the spirit affixed unto those elements and words, power of operation within the soul, most admirable, divine, and impossible to be expressed. For so God hath instituted and ordained, that, together with due administration and receipt of sacramental signs, there shall proceed from himself grace effectual to sanctify, to cure, to comfort, and whatsoever else is for the good of the souls of men.

Howbeit this opinion[1] Thomas rejecteth, under pretence that it maketh sacramental words and elements to be in themselves no more than signs, whereas they ought to be held as causes of that they signify. He therefore reformeth it with this addition, that the very sensible parts of the sacraments do instrumentally effect and produce, not grace, (for the schoolmen both of these times, and long after, did, for the most part, maintain it untrue, and some of them unpossible,[2] that sanctifying grace should efficiently proceed but from God alone, and that by immediate creation, as the substance of the soul doth;) but the phantasy which Thomas had was, that sensible things, through Christ's and the priest's benediction, receive a certain supernatural transitory force, which leaveth behind it a kind of preparative quality

---

[1] "Iste modus non transcendit rationem signi, cum sacramenta novæ legis non solum significent, sed, causent gratiam." Par. iii. q. 62. art. 1. Alexand. par. iv. q. 8. memb. 3. art. v. sect. 1 et 2. Th. de verit. q. 27. art. iii. Alliac. in quart. sent. ix. 1. Capr. in 4. d. 1. q. 1. Palud. Tom. Ferrar. lib. iv. cont. Gent. c. 57. " Necesse est ponere aliquam virtutem supernaturalem in sacramentis." Sent. iv. d. 1. q. 1. art. iv. " Sacramentum consequitur spiritualem virtutem cum benedictione Christi, et applicatione ministri ad usum sacramenti." Par. iii. q. 62. art. iv. Concil. " Victus sacramentalis habet esse transiens ex uno in aliud et incompletum." *Ibidem.* " Ex sacramentis duo consequuntur in anima, unum est character, sive aliquis ornatus ; aliud, est gratia. Respectu primo, sacramenta sunt causæ aliquo modo efficientes ; respectu secundo, sunt disponentes. Sacramenta causant dispositionem ad formam ultimam, sed ultimam perfectionem non inducunt." Sent. iv. d. 1. q. 1. art. iv.

[2] Unpossible: *i.e.* impossible.

or beauty within the soul, whereupon immediately from God doth ensue the grace that justifieth.

Now they which pretend to follow Thomas, differ from him in two points. For, first, they make grace an immediate effect of the outward sign, which he for the dignity and excellency thereof was afraid to do. Secondly, whereas he, to produce but a preparative quality in the soul, did imagine God to create in the instrument a supernatural gift or ability ; they confess, that nothing is created, infused, or any way inherent, either in the word or in the elements ; nothing that giveth them instrumental efficacy, but God's mere motion or application.[1] Are they able to explain unto us, or themselves to conceive, what they mean when they thus speak? For example, let them teach us, in the sacrament of baptism, what it is for water to be moved till it bring forth grace. The application thereof by the minister is plain to sense ; the force which it hath in the mind, as a moral instrument of information or instruction, we know by reason ; and by faith, we understand how God doth assist it with his Spirit : whereupon ensueth the grace which Saint Cyprian did in himself observe, saying,[2] "After the bath of regeneration having scoured out the stained foulness of former life, supernatural light had entrance into the breast which was purified and cleansed for it : after that a second nativity had made another man, by inward receipt of the Spirit from heaven ; things doubtful began in marvellous manner to appear certain, that to be open which lay hid, darkness to shine like a clear light, former hardness to be made facility, impossibility easiness : insomuch as it might be discerned how that was earthly,[3] which before had been carnally bred and lived, given over unto sins ; that now God's own, which the Holy Ghost did quicken."

---

[1] "Solus Deus efficit gratiam adeo quod nec angelis, qui sunt nobiliores sensibilibus creaturis, hoc communicetur." Bonav. Sent. iv. d. 1. q. 1. art. iv.

[2] Ad Donat. c. 3.

[3] We may be surprised at the word 'earthly." The Latin is, 'ut esset agnoscere terrenum fuisse, quod prius carnaliter natum delictis, obnoxium viveret." Perhaps we convey the idea of St. Cyprian best by a paraphrase, "fit to live on God's earth."

[11.] Our opinion is therefore plain unto every man's understanding. We take it for a very good speech which Bonaventure hath uttered in saying,[1] "Heed must be taken, that while we assign too much to the bodily signs in way of their commendation, we withdraw not the honour which is due to the cause which worketh in them, and the soul which receiveth them. Whereunto we conformably teach, that the outward sign applied hath of itself no natural efficacy towards grace, neither doth God put into it any supernatural inherent virtue." And, as I think, we thus far avouch no more than they themselves confess to be very true.

If anything displease them, it is because we add to these promises another assertion; that, with the outward sign, God joineth his Holy Spirit, and so the whole instrument of God bringeth that to pass, whereunto the baser and meaner part could not extend. As for operations through the motion of signs, they are dark, intricate, and obscure; perhaps possible, howbeit, not proved either true or likely, by alleging, that the touch of our Saviour's garment[2] restored health,[3] clay sight, when he applied it. Although ten thousand such examples should be brought, they overthrow not this one principle; that, where the instrument is without inherent virtue, the effect must necessarily proceed from the only agent's adherent power.

It passeth a man's conceit how water should be carried into the soul with any force of divine motion, or grace proceed but merely from the influence of God's Spirit. Notwithstanding, if God himself teach his Church in this case to believe that which he hath not given us capacity to comprehend, how incredible soever it may seem, yet our wits should submit themselves, and reason give place unto faith therein. But they[4] yield it to be

---

[1] "Cavendum enim ne dum nimis damus corporalibus signis ad laudem, subtrahamus honorem causæ curanti et animæ suscipienti." Bonav. Sent. iv. d. 1. q. 4. art. 1.

[2] Luke viii.
[3] John ix.
[4] Bellarm. de effect. Sacr. lib. ii. c. 1.

no question of faith, how grace doth proceed from sacraments; if in general they be acknowledged true instrumental causes, by the ministry whereof men receive divine grace,[1] and that[2] they which impute grace to the only operation of God himself, concurring with the external sign, do no less acknowledge the true efficacy of the sacrament, than they that ascribe the same to the quality of the sign applied, or to the motion of God applying, and so far carrying it, till grace be thereby not created, but extracted, out of the natural possibility of the soul. Nevertheless, this last philosophical imagination, (if I may call it philosophical, which useth the terms, but overthroweth the rules of philosophy, and hath no article of faith to support it,) but whatsoever it be, they follow it in a manner all; they cast off the first opinion, wherein is most perspicuity and strongest evidence of certain truth.

The council[3] of Florence and Trent defining, that sacraments contain and confer grace, the sense whereof (if it liked them) might so easily conform itself with the same opinion which[4] they drew without any just cause quite and clean the other way, making grace the issue of bare words, in such sacraments as they have framed destitute of any visible element, and holding it the offspring as well of elements as of words in those sacraments where both are; but in no sacrament acknowledging grace to be the fruit of the Holy Ghost working with the outward sign, and not by it, in such sort as Thomas himself teacheth;[5] that the Apostles' imposition of hands caused not the coming of the Holy Ghost,

---

[1] "Dicimus gratiam non creari a Deo, sed produci ex aptitudine et potentia naturali animæ, sicut cætera omnia quæ producuntur in subjectis talibus, quæ sunt apta nata ad suscipiendum accidentia." Allen. de Sacr. in Gen. c. 37.

[2] I have followed here, the punctuation of C. and P., which gives a clearer meaning.

[3] Query: "councils."

[4] "The obvious corruption of the text here may perhaps be rightly removed by leaving out the word 'which.'" (C. and P.) If this be so, a comma should be placed after "opinion."

[5] Thom. de Verit. q. 27. art. 3. resp. ad 16.

Ch. vi. § 11. which notwithstanding was bestowed together with the exercise of that ceremony; yea, by it, (saith the Evangelist,)[1] to wit, as by a mean which came between the true agent and the effect, but not otherwise.

Many of the ancient Fathers, presupposing that the faithful before Christ had not, till the time of his coming, that perfect life and salvation which they looked for and we possess, thought likewise their sacraments to be but prefigurations of that which ours in present do exhibit. For which cause the Florentine council, comparing the one with the other, saith,[2] "That the old did only shadow grace, which was afterwards to be given through the passion of Jesus Christ." But the after-wit of latter days hath found out another more exquisite distinction, that evangelical sacraments are causes to effect grace, through motions of signs legal, according to the same signification and sense wherein evangelical sacraments are held by us to be God's instruments for that purpose. For howsoever Bellarmine hath shrunk up the Lutherans' sinews, and cut off our doctrine by the skirts;[3] Allen,

---

[1] Acts viii. 18.

[2] T. xiii. 534. "Illa non causabant gratiam, sed eam solum per passionem Christi dandam esse figurabant." (C. and P.)

[3] "Quod ad circumcisionem sequebatur remissio, fiebat ratione, rei adjunctæ et ratione pacti divini, eodem plane modo quo non solum hæretici, sed etiam aliquot vetustiores scholastici voluerunt nova sacramenta conferre gratiam." Allen. de Sacr. in Gen. c. 39. "Bonaventura, Scotus, Durandus, Richardus, Occamus, Marsilius, Gabriel,—volunt solum Deum producere gratiam ad præsentiam sacramentorum. Bellarm. de Sacr. in Gen. lib. ii. c. 11. "Puto longe probabiliorem et tutiorem sententiam quæ dat sacramentis veram efficientiam. Primo quia doctores passim docent, sacramenta non agere nisi prius a Deo virtutem seu benedictionem seu sanctificationem accipiant, et referunt effectum sacramentorum ad omnipotentiam Dei, et conferunt cum veris causis efficientibus. Secundo, quia non esset differentia inter modum agendi Sacramentorum, et signorum magicorum. Tertio, quia tunc non esset homo Dei minister in ipsa actione Sacramentali, sed homo præberet signum actione sua, et Deus alia actione, viso eo signo, infunderet gratiam, ut cum unus ostendit syngrapham mercatori, et ille dat pecunias. At Scripturæ docent, quod Deus baptizat per hominem." Bellarm. lib. ii. cap. 11.

although he term us heretics, acording to the usual bitter venom of 'his first style, doth yet ingenuously confess, that the old schoolmen's doctrine and ours is one concerning sacramental efficacy, derived from God himself, assisting by promise those outward signs of elements and words, out of which their schoolmen of the newer mint are so desirous to hatch grace. Where God doth work and use these outward means, wherein he neither findeth nor planteth force and aptness towards his intended purpose; such means are but signs to bring men to the consideration of his omnipotent power, which, without the use of things sensible, would not be marked.

At the time, therefore, when he giveth his heavenly grace, he applieth, by the hands of his ministers, that which betokeneth the same; not only betokeneth, but, being also accompanied for ever with such power as doth truly work, is in that respect termed God's instrument, a true efficient cause of grace; a cause not in itself, but only by connexion of that which is in itself a cause, namely, God's own strength and power. Sacraments, that is to say, the outward signs in sacraments, work nothing till they be blessed and sanctified by God.

But what is God's heavenly benediction and sanctification, saving only the association of his Spirit? Shall we say that sacraments are like magical signs, if thus they have their effect? Is it magic for God to manifest by things sensible what he doth, and to do by His own most glorious Spirit really, what he manifesteth in his sacraments? The delivery and administration whereof remaineth in the hands of mortal men, by whom, as by personal instruments, God doth apply signs, and with signs inseparably join his Spirit, and through the power of his Spirit work grace.[1] The first is by way of concomitance and consequence to deliver the rest also that either accompany or ensue.

---

[1] *i.e.* (to illustrate by one sacrament) the elements in the Lord's Supper, as faithfully received, are accompanied by God's Holy Spirit, and are outward signs of grace certainly given to, and surely working in, the believer, through the power of the Spirit.

Ch. vi. §. 12.   It is not here, as in cases of mutual commerce, where divers persons have divers acts to be performed in their own behalf; a creditor to show his bill, and a debtor to pay his money. But God and man do here meet in one action upon a third, in whom, as it is the work of God to create grace, so it is his work by the hand of the ministry to apply a sign which should betoken, and his work to annex that Spirit which shall effect it. The action, therefore, is but one, God the author thereof, and man a co-partner, by him assigned to work for, with, and under him. God the Giver of grace by the outward ministry of man, so far forth as he authorizeth man to apply the sacraments of grace in the soul, which he alone worketh, without either instrument or co-agent.

[12.] Whereas, therefore, with us the remission of sin is ascribed unto God, as a thing which proceedeth from him only, and presently followeth upon the virtue of true repentance appearing in man; that which we attribute to the virtue, they do not only impute to the sacrament of repentance, but having made repentance a sacrament, and thinking of sacraments as they do, they are enforced to make the ministry of the priests, and their absolution, a cause of that which the sole omnipotency of God worketh.

And yet, for my own part, I am not able well to conceive how their doctrine, that human absolution is really a cause out of which our deliverance from sin doth ensue, can cleave with the council of Trent, defining,[1] "That contrition perfected with charity doth at all times itself reconcile offenders to God, before they come to receive actually the sacrament of penance." How can it stand with those discourses of the learned rabbins, which grant,[2] "That whosoever turneth unto God with his whole heart, hath immediately his sins taken away; that if a man be truly converted, his pardon can neither be denied nor delayed?" it doth not stay for the priest's absolution, but presently followeth. Surely, if every contrite sinner, in whom there is charity and a sincere

---

[1] Conc. Trid. Sess. xiv. c. 4.   [2] Bellarm. de Pœn. lib. ii. c. 13.

conversion of heart, have remission of sins given him before he seek it at the priest's hands; if reconciliation to God be a present and immediate sequel upon every such conversion or change; it must of necessity follow, seeing no man can be a true penitent or contrite which doth not both love God and sincerely abhor sin, that therefore they all before absolution attain forgiveness; whereunto notwithstanding absolution is pretended a cause so necessary, that sin without it, except in some rare extraordinary case, cannot possibly be remitted. Shall absolution be a cause producing and working that effect which is always brought forth without it, and had before absolution be thought of? But, when they which are thus beforehand pardoned of God shall come to be also assoiled by the priest, I would know what force his absolution hath in this case? Are they able to say here, that the priest doth remit any thing? Yet, when any of ours ascribeth the work of remission to God, and interpreteth the priest's sentence to be but a solemn declaration of that which God himself hath already performed, they scorn at it; they urge against it, that if this were true, our Saviour Christ should rather have said, "What is loosed in heaven, ye shall loose on earth," than as He doth, "Whatsoever ye loose on earth shall in heaven be loosed." As if he were to learn of us how to place his words, and not we to crave rather of him a sound and right understanding, lest to his dishonour and our own hurt we misexpound them. It sufficeth, I think, both against their constructions to have proved that they ground an untruth on his speech, and, in behalf of our own, that his words without any such transposition do very well admit the sense we give them; which is, that he taketh to himself the lawful proceedings of authority in his name, and that the act of spiritual authority in this case is by sentence to acquit or pronounce them free from sin whom they judge to be sincerely and truly penitent; which interpretation they themselves do acknowledge, though not sufficient, yet very true.[1]

[1] "Hæc expositio, Ego te absolvo, id est, Absolutum ostendo, partim quidem vera est, non tamen perfecta. Sacra-

Of Absolution by the Popish Priest

Absolution, they say, declareth indeed, but this is not all, for it likewise maketh innocent, which addition being an untruth proved, our truth granted hath, I hope, sufficiency without it, and consequently our opinion therein neither to be challenged as untrue, nor as unsufficient.

[13.] To rid themselves out of these briers, and to make remission of sins an effect of absolution, notwithstanding that which hitherto hath been said, they have two shifts. As first, that in many penitents there is but [1] attrition of heart, which attrition they define to be grief proceeding from fear without love; and to these, they say, absolution doth give that contrition whereby men are really purged from sin. Secondly, that even where contrition or inward repentance doth cleanse without absolution; the reason why it cometh so to pass is,[2] because such contrites intend and desire absolution, though they have it not. Which two things granted: the one, that absolution given maketh them contrite that are not; the other, even in them which are contrite, the cause why God remitteth sin is the purpose or desire they have to receive absolution:[3] we are not to stand against a sequel so clear and manifest as this, that always remission of sin proceedeth from absolution either had or desired.

But should a reasonable man give credit to their bare conceit, and because their positions have driven them to imagine absolving of unsufficiently-disposed penitents to be a real creating of further virtue in them, must all other men think it due? Let them cancel henceforward and blot out of all their books those old cautions touch-

menta quippe novæ legis non solum significant, sed efficiunt quod significant." Soto, sent. i. iv. dis. 14, q. 1. art. 3.

[1] "Attritio solum dicit dolorem propter pœnas inferri; dum quis accedit attritus, per gratiam sacramentalem fit contritus." Soto, sent. iv. dis. 14, q. 1. art. 1.

[2] "Dam accedit vere contritus propter Deum, illa etiam contritio non est contritio, nisi quatenus prius natura informetur gratiâ per sacramentum in voto." Soto, sent. iv. dis. 14, q. 1. art. 1.

[3] "Legitima contritio votum sacramenti pro suo tempore debet inducere, atque adeo in virtute futuri sacramenti peccata remittit." *Ibid.* art. 3.

Absurdity of limiting Pardon to Desire of Absolution

ing necessity of wisdom,[1] lest priests should inconsiderately absolve any man in whom there were not apparent tokens of true repentance;[2] which to do was, in St. Cyprian's judgment,[3] "pestilent deceit and flattery, not only not available, but hurtful to them that had transgressed: a frivolous, frustrate, and false peace, such as caused the unrighteous to trust to a lie, and destroyed them unto whom it promised safety." What needeth observation whether penitents have worthiness and bring contrition, if the words of absolution do infuse contrition? Have they borne us all this while in hand that contrition is a part of the matter of their sacraments; a condition or preparation of the mind towards grace to be received by absolution in the form of their sacraments? And must we now believe that the form doth give the matter? That absolution bestoweth contrition, and that the words do make presently of Saul, David; of Judas, Peter? For what was the penitency of Saul and Judas, but plain attrition; horror of sin through fear of punishment, without any loving sense, or taste of God's mercy?

Their other fiction, imputing remission of sin to desire of absolution from the priest, even in them which are truly contrite, is an evasion somewhat more witty, but no whit more possible for them to prove. Belief of the world and judgment to come, faith in the promises and sufferings of Christ for mankind, fear of his majesty, love of his mercy, grief for sin, hope for pardon, suit for grace—these we know to be elements of true contrition: suppose that besides all this, God did also command that every penitent should seek his absolution at the priest's hands; where so many causes are concurring unto one effect, have they any reason to impute the whole effect unto one? any reason in the choice of

---

[1] "Tunc sententia sacerdotis judicio Dei et totius cœlestis curiæ approbatur, et confirmatur, cum ita ex discretione procedit, ut reorum merita non contradicant." Sent. :. iv. d. 18.

[2] "Non est periculosum sacerdoti dicere, Ego te absolvo, illis in quibus signa contritionis videt, quæ sunt dolor de præteritis, et propositum de cætero non peccandi; alios absolvere non debet." Tho. Opusc. 22.

[3] De Laps. p. 127.

Ch. vi. § 13. that one, to pass by faith, fear, love, humility, hope, prayer, whatsoever else, and to enthronize above them all a desire of absolution from the priest, as if, in the whole work of man's repentance, God did regard and accept nothing, but for and in consideration of this? Why do the Tridentine council [1] impute it to charity "That contrites are reconciled in God's sight before they receive the sacrament of penance," if desired absolution be the true cause?

But let this pass how it will; seeing the question is not what virtue God may accept in penitent sinners, but what grace absolution actually given doth really bestow upon them. If it were, as they would have it, that God, regarding the humiliation of a contrite spirit, because there is joined therewith a lowly desire of the sacrament of priestly absolution, pardoneth immediately and forgiveth all offences; doth this any thing help to prove that absolution received afterwards from the priest, can more than declare him already pardoned which did desire it? To desire absolution, presupposing it commanded, is obedience; and obedience in that case is a branch of the virtue of repentance; which virtue being thereby made effectual to the taking away of sins without the sacrament of repentance, is it not an argument that the sacrament of absolution hath here no efficacy, but the virtue of contrition worketh all? For how should any effect ensue from causes which actually are not? The sacrament must be applied wheresoever any grace doth proceed from it. So that where it is but desired only, whatsoever may follow upon God's acceptation of this desire, the sacrament, afterwards received, can be no cause thereof. Wherefore the further we wade, the better we see it still appear, that the priest doth never in absolution, no not so much as by way of service and ministry, really either forgive them, take away the uncleanness, or remove the punishment of sin: but, if the party penitent become contrite, he hath, by their own grant, absolution before absolution; if not

---

[1] Sess. xiv. c. 4

Not the Priest's Absolution, but Contrition effective

contrite, although the priest should seem a thousand times to absolve him, all were in vain. For which cause the ancients and better sort of their school-divines, [1]Abulensis, [2]Alexander Hales, and [3]Bonaventure ascribe "the real abolition of sin, and eternal punishment, to the mere pardon of Almighty God, without dependency upon the priest's absolution, as a cause to effect the same": his absolution hath in their doctrine certain other effects specified, but this denied. Wherefore having hitherto spoken of the virtue of repentance required; of the discipline of repentance which Christ did establish; and of the sacrament of repentance invented sithence,[4] against the pretended force of human absolution in sacramental penitency; let it suffice thus far to have shewed how God alone doth truly give, the virtue of repentance alone procure, and private ministerial absolution but declare, remission of sins.

[14.] Now the last and sometimes hardest to be satisfied by repentance, are our minds; and our minds we have then satisfied, when the conscience is of guilty[5] become clear. For, as long as we are in ourselves privy to our own most heinous crimes, but without sense of God's

---

[1] "A reatu mortis æternæ absolvitur homo a Deo per contritionem; manet autem reatus ad quandam pœnam temporalem, et minister ecclesiæ quicunque virtute clavium tollit reatum cujusdam partis pœnæ illius." Abul. in defens. p. i. c. 7.

[2] "Signum hujus sacramenti est causa effectiva gratiæ sive remissionis peccatorum; non simpliciter, sicut ipsa prima pœnitentia, sed secundum quid; quia est causa efficaciæ gratiæ qua fit remissio peccati, quantum ad aliquem effectum in pœnitente, ad minus quantum ad remissionem sequelæ ipsius peccati, scilicet pœnæ." Alex. p. iv. q. 14. memb.

[3] "Potestas clavium proprie loquendo non se extendit supra culpam: ad illud quod objicitur, Joan. 20. Quorum remiseritis peccata; dicendum, quod vel illud de remissione dicitur quantum ad offensionem, vel solum quantum ad pœnam." Bon. sent. l. i. d. 18. q. 1. "Ab æterna pœna nullo modo solvit sacerdos, sed a purgatorio; neque hoc per se, sed per accidens, quod cum in pœnitente, virtute clavium, minuitur debitum pœnæ temporalis, non ita acriter punietur in purgatorio, sicut si non esset absolutus." Sent. l. iv. d. 18. q. 2.

[4] Sithence: *i.e.* Since.

[5] Of guilty: *i.e.* from being guilty.

mercy and grace towards us, unless the heart be either brutish for want of knowledge, or altogether hardened by wilful atheism, the remorse of sin is in it, as the deadly sting of the serpent. Which point since very infidels and heathens have observed in the nature of sin, (for the disease they felt, though they knew no remedy to help it,) we are not rashly to despise those sentences which are the testimonies of their experience touching this point. They knew that the eye of a man's own conscience is more to be feared by evil-doers than the presence of a thousand witnesses, inasmuch as the mouths of other accusers are many ways stopped, the ears of the accused not always subject to glowing with contumely and exprobration; whereas a guilty mind being forced to be still both a martyr and a tyrant in itself, must of necessity endure perpetual anguish and grief; for as the body is rent with stripes, so the mind with guiltiness of cruelty, lust, and wicked resolutions. Which furies brought the emperor Tiberius sometimes into such perplexity, that writing to the senate, his wonted art of dissimulation failed him utterly in this case; and whereas it had been ever his peculiar delight so to speak that no man might be able to sound his meaning, he had not the power to conceal what he felt through the secret scourge of an evil conscience, though no necessity did now enforce him to disclose the same.[1] "What to write, or how to write, at this present, if I know, (saith Tiberius,) let the gods and goddesses, who thus continually eat me, only be worse to me than they are." It was not his imperial dignity and power, that could provide a way to protect him against himself; the fears and suspicions which improbity had bred being strengthened by every occasion, and those virtues clean banished which are the only foundation of sound tranquillity of mind. For which cause it hath been truly said, and agreeably with all men's experience, that if the virtuous did excel in no other privilege, yet far happier they are than the contrary sort of men, for that their hopes be always better.

[1] Tacit Annal. lib. vi. c. 6.

Neither are we to marvel, that these things, known unto all, do stay so few from being authors of their own woe.

For we see by the ancient example of Joseph's unkind brethren, how it cometh to remembrance easily when crimes are once past, what the difference is of good from evil, and of right from wrong: but such considerations, when they should have prevented sin, were overmatched by inordinate desires. Are we not bound then with all thankfulness to acknowledge his infinite goodness and mercy, which have revealed unto us the way how to rid ourselves of these mazes; the way how to shake off that yoke, which no flesh is able to bear; the way how to change most grisly horror into a comfortable apprehension of heavenly joy?

[15.] Whereunto there are many which labour with so much the greater difficulty, because imbecility[1] of mind doth not suffer them to censure rightly their own doings. Some fearful lest the enormity of their crimes be so unpardonable that no repentance can do them good; some lest the imperfection of their repentance make it uneffectual to the taking away of sin. The one drive all things to this issue, whether they be not men that have sinned against the Holy Ghost; the other to this, what repentance is sufficient to clear sinners, and to assure them that they are delivered.

Such as by error charge themselves of unpardonable sin, must think, it may be they deem that impardonable which is not.

Our Saviour speaketh indeed of blasphemy which shall never be forgiven; but have they any sure and infallible knowledge what that blasphemy is? If not, why are they unjust and cruel to their own souls, imagining certainty of guiltiness in a crime concerning the very nature whereof they are uncertain? For mine own part, although, where this blasphemy is mentioned, the cause why our Saviour spake thereof, was the Pharisees' blasphemy, which was not afraid to say,[2] "He had an

---

[1] Imbecility: *i.e.* weakness.   [2] Matt. ix. 34; Mark iii. 22.

Ch. vi. § 15. unclean spirit, and did cast out spirits by the power of Beelzebub"; nevertheless I dare not precisely deny, but that even the Pharisees themselves might have repented and been forgiven, and that our Lord Jesus Christ peradventure might but take occasion at their blasphemy, which, as yet, was pardonable, to tell them further of an unpardonable blasphemy, whereinto he foresaw that the Jews would fall. For it is plain, that many thousands, at the first professing the Christian religion, became afterwards wilful apostates, moved with no other cause of revolt, but mere indignation that the Gentiles should enjoy the benefit of the Gospel as much as they, and yet not be burdened with the yoke of Moses' law.

The Apostles by preaching had won them to Christ, in whose name they embraced with great alacrity the full remission of their former sins and iniquities; they received by the imposition of the Apostles' hands[1] that grace and power of the Holy Ghost whereby they cured diseases, prophesied, spake with tongues: and yet in the end, after all this, they fell utterly away, renounced the mysteries of Christian faith, blasphemed in their formal abjurations that most glorious and blessed Spirit, the gifts whereof themselves had possessed; and by this means sunk their souls in the gulf of that unpardonable sin, whereof as our Lord Jesus Christ had told them beforehand, so the Apostle at the first appearance of such their revolt, putteth them in mind again,[2] that falling now to their former blasphemies, their salvation was irrecoverably gone. It was for them in this case impossible to be renewed by any repentance; because they were now in the state of Satan and his angels; the Judge of quick and dead had passed his irrevocable sentence against them.

So great difference there is between infidels unconverted, and backsliders in this manner fallen away, that always we have hope to reclaim the one which only hate whom they never knew; but to the other which know and blaspheme, to them that with more than infernal

---

[1] Acts ii. 38. [2] Heb. vi. 6.

malice accurse both the seen brightness of glory which is in him, and in themselves the tasted goodness of divine grace, as those execrable miscreants did, who first received in extraordinary miraculous manner,[1] and then in outrageous sort blasphemed the Holy Ghost, abusing both it and the whole religion, which God by it did confirm and magnify; to such as wilfully thus sin, after so great light and the truth and gifts of the Spirit, there remaineth justly no fruit or benefit to be expected by Christ's sacrifice.

For all other offenders, without exception or stint, whether they be strangers that seek access, or followers that will make return unto God; upon the tender of their repentance, the grant of his grace standeth everlastingly signed with his blood in the book of eternal life. That which in this case over-terrifieth fearful souls is a misconceit whereby they imagine every act which they do, knowing that they do amiss, and every wilful breach or transgression of God's law, to be mere sin against the Holy Ghost; forgetting that the law of Moses itself ordained sacrifices of expiation, as well for faults presumptuously committed, as things wherein men offend by error.

[16.] Now, there are on the contrary side others, who, doubting not of God's mercy towards all that perfectly repent, remain notwithstanding scrupulous and troubled with continual fear, lest defects in their own repentance be a bar against them.

These cast themselves into very great, and peradventure needless, agonies,[2] through misconstruction of things spoken about proportioning our griefs to our sins,[3] for which they never think they have wept and

---

[1] Heb. x. 26.
[2] Jer. vi. 26; Micah i. 8, 9; Lam. ii. 18.
[3] "Quam magna delinquimus, tam granditer defleamus. Alto vulneri diligens et longa medicina non desit; pœnitentia crimine minor non sit." Cypr. de Laps. p. 137. "Non levi agendum est contritione, ut debita illa redimantur, quibus mors æterna debetur; nec transitora opus est satisfactione pro malis illis, propter quæ paratus est ignis æternus." Euseb. Emisenus, vel potius Salv. f. 106.

mourned enough, yea, if they have not always a stream of tears at command, they take it for a heart congealed and hardened in sin; when to keep the wound of contrition bleeding, they unfold the circumstances of their transgressions, and endeavour to leave out nothing which may be heavy against themselves.

Yet, do what they can, they are still fearful, lest herein also they do not that which they ought and might. Come to prayer, their coldness taketh all heart and courage from them; with fasting, albeit their flesh should be withered, and their blood clean dried up, would they ever the less object, What is this to David's humiliation?[1] wherein notwithstanding there was not any thing more than necessary. In works of charity and alms-deed, it is not all the world can persuade them they did ever reach the poor bounty of the widow's two mites,[2] or by many millions of leagues come near to the mark which Cornelius touched;[3] so far they are off from the proud surmise of any penitential supererogation in miserable wretched worms of the earth.

Notwithstanding, forasmuch as they wrong themselves with over rigorous and extreme exactions, by means whereof they fall sometimes into such perplexities as can hardly be allayed; it hath therefore pleased Almighty God, in tender commiseration over these imbecilities of men, to ordain for their spiritual and ghostly comfort consecrated persons, which by sentence of power and authority given from above, may, as it were, out of his very mouth ascertain[4] timorous and doubtful minds in their own particular, ease them of all their scrupulosities, leave them settled in peace and satisfied touching the mercy of God towards them. To use the benefit of this help for the better satisfaction in such cases is so natural, that it can be forbidden no man; but yet not so necessary, that all men should be in case to need it.

[17.] They are, of the two, the happier, therefore, that can content and satisfy themselves, by judging

---

[1] Psalm vi. 6.
[2] Mark xii. 42.
[3] Acts. x. 31.
[4] Ascertain: *i.e.* assure.

discreetly what they perform, and soundly what God doth require of them. For having that which is most material, the substance of penitency rightly bred ; touching signs and tokens thereof, we may affirm that they do boldly, which imagine for every offence a certain proportionable degree in the passions and griefs of mind, whereunto whosoever aspireth not, repenteth in vain.

That to frustrate men's confession and considerations of sin, except every circumstance which may aggravate the same be unript and laid in the balance, is a merciless extremity ; although it be true, that as near as we can such wounds must be searched to the very bottom. Last of all, to set down the like stint, and to shut up the doors of mercy against penitents which come short thereof in the devotion of their prayers, in the continuance of their fasts, in the largeness and bounty of their alms, or in the course of any other such like duties ; is more than God himself hath thought meet, and consequently more than mortal men should presume to do.

That which God doth chiefly respect in men's penitency is their hearts.[1] " The heart is it which maketh repentance sincere," sincerity that which findeth favour in God's sight, and the favour of God that which supplieth by gracious acceptation whatsoever may seem defective in the faithful, hearty, and true offices of his servants.

Take it (saith Chrysostom) upon my credit,[2] " Such is God's merciful inclination towards men, that repentance offered with a single and sincere mind he never refuseth; no, not although we be come to the very top of iniquity." If there be a will and desire to return, he receiveth, embraceth, and omitteth nothing which may restore us to former happiness ; yea, that which is yet above all the rest, albeit we cannot, in the duty of satisfying him, attain what we ought, and would, but come far behind our mark, he taketh nevertheless in good worth that little which we do ; be it never so mean, we lose not our labour therein.

[1] Jer. xxix. 13 ; Joel ii. 12.
[2] Chrys. de repar. lapsis. lib. ad Theodor. de Pœnit. dis. 3. c. *Talis.*

Ch. vi. § 17. The least and lowest step of repentance, in St. Chrysostom's judgment, serveth and setteth us above them that perish in their sin : I therefore will end with St. Augustine's conclusion,[1] "Lord, in thy book and volume of life all shall be written, as well the least of thy saints, as the chiefest." Let not therefore the unperfect fear; let them only proceed and go forward.

[1] Aug. in Psal. cxxxviii.

APPENDIX.

NOTES UPON SOME OF THE WRITERS AND EVENTS REFERRED TO BY RICHARD HOOKER IN THE SIXTH BOOK OF THE *Ecclesiastical Polity.*

Abulensis. (Chapter vi. § 13.)

The reference is to Tostatus, who was bishop of Avila circ. 1400–1455. [C. and P.]

Alexander Hales. (Chapter vi. § 13.)

Alexander of Hales, or Ales—also called Alexander Alesius—from the name of his birthplace, near Gloucester. He studied at Paris, where he quickly became one of the most famous teachers, at the most brilliant epoch of the scholastic philosophy. St. Bonaventure was one of his pupils. (See below, Bonaventure.) He died at Paris in 1245. His great work is a *Summa Theologiæ*. He was surnamed, in the Middle Ages, "Infallible Doctor," and "Fountain of Light."

Allen. (Chapter vi. § 11.)

John Allen, D.D., archbishop of Dublin, to which See he was promoted in 1528. He was educated at Oxford, and in 1515 was employed by Warham, archbishop of Canterbury, as his agent to the See of Rome, where he resided nine years. On his return, he became chaplain to Wolsey, and was one of his chief abettors in procuring the dissolution of some of the lesser monasteries, for the foundation of the Cardinal's colleges at Oxford and Ipswich.

Ambrose, Saint. (Chapter iv. §§ 5, 6, 14, 15.)

Born at Treves A.D. 340, and brought up to the legal profession; but having been appointed consular prefect of Liguria, the province in which Milan was situated, and being engaged in preservin peace at an election of a successor to Auxentius, archbishop of that city, he was himself chosen by popular acclamation to that office, and consecrated on the eighth day after his baptism. A striking incident of his life is his compelling the Roman emperor Theodosius to undergo public penance in his cathedral. His treatises on Faith and on the Holy Spirit were composed for the instruction of the youthful emperor Gratian; but, to judge from his writings, the chief subject which occupied his attention was the spiritual direction of virgins and widows. His book on *Virgins* was written within two years of his consecration, and is dedicated to his sister Marcellina.

Augustine, Saint. (Chapter v. § 4.)

St. Augustine, the most eminent of the Latin Fathers, was bishop of Hippo. He was born 354 A.D., and died in 430, at the age of 76. We need not say more of him here, than that he was 53 years old before he embraced Christianity; that his *Confessions* give a most graphic account of his own spiritual experiences; that his work *De Civitate Dei* is an elaborate defence of Christianity, and perhaps his greatest production; and that he may be looked upon as the father of the theology of the Reformation. "The light that was in him was not extinguished by his death, but only ascended to a higher place, and has been shining through the centuries ever since." (Dr. Lindsay Alexander.)

Baronius. (Chapter iv. § 10.)

Cæsar Baronius, the famous historian and cardinal, was born at Sora, in Naples, A.D. 1538; made cardinal in 1596; died 1607. The great work of Baronius, his *Annales Ecclesiastici*—to which no doubt Hooker alludes—was the labour of thirty years. It was published in twelve volumes, the first of which appeared in 1588, and the last in 1607, the year of his death.

Basil, Saint. (Chapter iii. § 3.)

Surnamed "the Great"; born at Cæsarea, in Cappadocia, A.D. 329. He was ordained deacon in 357, and priest some years afterwards. Always inclined to monastic life, he visited various places to perfect himself in the necessary discipline, and founded a monastery near his native city. In 370 he was made archbishop of Cæsarea, where he strongly resisted the emperor Valens in his attempts to introduce the Arian heresy into the Church. He was held in the highest estimation by his flock. His works were very numerous, and his style is described as "admirable, perspicuous, and powerful, flowing with unaffected grace and natural sweetness."

Bellarmine. (Chapter iv. § 5.)

Cardinal Robert Francis Romulus Bellarmine, one of the greatest of Roman Catholic polemical divines, was born at Montepulciano, in Tuscany, October 4, 1542. After studying at the University of Padua, he entered the order of the Jesuits, and lectured with success at Louvain and Ghent. He next proceeded to Rome, where he taught in the newly-founded Collegium Romanum. For many years, after the publication of his *Disputationes de Controversiis Christianæ Fidei*, he was looked upon as the champion of the papacy, and a vindication of Protestantism regularly took the shape of an answer to Bellarmine. He was made a cardinal in 1599, and in 1602 became archbishop of Capua. He died in the Jesuit College at Rome, 27th September, 1621. It will be seen from the above notes that Cardinal Bellarmine was contemporary with Richard Hooker, and survived him more than twenty years.

Bonaventure. (Chapter vi. §§ 11, 13.)

Giovanni de Fidenza, canonized under the name of Bonaventure, is said to have owed his name to an incident of his childhood. The prayers of St. Francis of Assisi had been invoked for him in some illness; and upon seeing him recovering, the aged monk exclaimed, "O buona ventura" (what good fortune)! He was born at Bagnarea, in Tuscany, 1221; entered the order of Franciscan monks, 1243; studied in Paris under Alexander Hales (see above, Alexander Hales); and having taken his doctor's degree, was chosen public lecturer on the "Sentences" of Peter Lombard (see below, Peter Lombard). He died at Lyons (while attending the council of Lyons) in July, 1274. He was canonized by Pope Sixtus IV. in 1472, and in 1587 was, by Pope Sixtus V., advanced to the dignity of fifth doctor of the Church. He was the rival in scholastic reputation of the Dominican, Thomas Aquinas; and his works are characterized by a devotional spirit of a fervour and pathos amply recognised by the fathers of the Reformation.

Cajetan. (Chapter iv. § 5.)

Cardinal Cajetan, whose real name was Thomas de Vio, took the name by which he is best known, from Cajeta, in the kingdom of Naples, where he was born in 1469. He was a distinguished member of the Dominican order, and held the office of general for ten years. He was made bishop of Cajeta, then archbishop of Palermo, and in 1517 was elevated to a place in the College of Cardinals. In the year following he was sent into Germany to combat Luther, and it was at his summons that the reformer appeared at Augsburg. Cardinal Cajetan wrote, amongst other works, a commentary on the theology of Thomas Aquinas. He died in 1534.

Calvin. (Chapter iv. § 14.)

The reference in this chapter to "the learneder sort of divines in reformed Churches," will in all probability be to John Calvin, a passage in his *Institutes* being named in the margin. Calvin was born 1509, and died May 27th, 1564. He has been described as the divine and dialectician of the Reformation, as Luther was its orator, and Melanchthon its scholar. The *Institutes* were published at Basle in 1536. The work is wonderful, not only for its style and form, but its lucid and logical arrangements, and for the influence which it has exerted on the age which produced it, and on succeeding centuries.

Cassianus. (Chapter iii. § 3 ; iv. § 13.)

His real name was Jean Cassian. He was born about A.D. 350, and resided chiefly at Marseilles, where he founded the famous abbey of St. Victor, where he died in 443. He was ordained deacon at Constantinople by St. Chrysostom, and obtained priest's orders at Marseilles. He founded two monasteries—one for men, the other for women ; the former, it is said, contained 5,000 monks. His chief works are his *Monastic Institutions* and his *Twenty-four Conferences of the Fathers of the Desert;* these were translated into French by Nicolas Fontaine. He also wrote a treatise on the Incarnation, directed against the Nestorian heresy.

Chrysostom, Saint. (Chapter iv. §§ 4, 13.)

The "golden-mouthed" bishop of Constantinople, born at Antioch 347 A.D. ; consecrated as bishop 398, on the death of Nectarius (see below). An unsparing reformer, he was met in certain quarters with bitter opposition, and was deposed by the so-called "Synod of the Oak" in 403. Recalled in a few days to Constantinople, he still set himself to resist the idolatrous festivities which he found to be carried on, and was deposed from his office for the second time in the year following (404), and banished to Cacusus, on the borders of Armenia. His place of banishment was presently changed to a little town named Pityus, in Pontus, near the eastern border of the Euxine Sea. On his way thither, however, he died at Comanum, in Pontus, September 14, 407. Chrysostom was the most eloquent, though not the most learned, of the Fathers. Dr. Samuel Davidson tells us that he had not, perhaps, "any equal in the use of that impassioned eloquence which befits the pulpit, till the time of Jeremy Taylor." "The epithet of Chrysostom, or 'golden-mouthed,' was not given him until after his death. It is an honourable and just tribute to his oratory."

Cyprian, Saint. (Chapter iv. § 6.)

A distinguished bishop of North Africa, born at the commencement of the third century, probably at Carthage. He was, in the year 248, chosen bishop of Carthage—not without much opposition from some of the elder presbyters. His severe and rigorous character as a disciplinarian brought him also into collision with the corrupt clergy of his diocese. In the Decian persecution (250) Cyprian was selected as a victim, the cry of the multitude being "Cyprianum ad leonem." This danger he avoided by flight, but returned to Carthage in 251, and shewed himself an admirable bishop, especially in the time of a pestilence which ravaged the city. Other chief events in his life were his controversy with the bishop of Rome concerning the baptism of heretics; his sufferings, together with the other African Christians, under the persecution of Valerian; and his martyrdom, by order of the pro-consul Aspasius Paternus, 14th September, 258, upon his refusal to sacrifice to the Roman gods. The life of St. Cyprian was a special study of the late Archbishop Benson, whose history of the life and times of St. Cyprian was published after his own death.

Duns Scotus. (Chapter iv. § 3.)

A scholastic divine, born about 1265, educated at Merton College, Oxford. Eminent for his talents and abilities, he was for a short time professor of theology at Oxford, but removed to Paris in 1301, where he occupied a similar position. It was Duns Scotus who first inculcated the doctrine of the "immaculate conception," on which occasion the title of "Subtle Doctor" was conferred upon him. He died suddenly of apoplexy in 1308. He was the head of the party of the Scotists against the Thomists, or followers of Thomas Aquinas. One of the best amongst the works of Duns Scotus is his questions or commentaries upon the Sentences of Peter Lombard, to which several references will be found in the notes to the Sixth Book of the *Polity*.

Durandus. (Chapter iv. § 3.)

Durand, a learned French Benedictine, was born about 1012 at Neubourg, and died in 1089. At a very early age he entered the monastery of Mont St. Catherine of Rouen. He was presently placed at the head of the Abbaye de St. Martin de Trouarn, in the diocese of Bayeux. The only one of Durand's works now extant is his dogmatic treatise *Of the Body and Blood of Jesus Christ, against Beringer and his Opponents*.

Eudæmon. (Chapter iv. § 10.)

A native of Alexandria, but a priest in the Church of Constantinople. He appears as the adviser of Nectarius, bishop of Constantinople, in the matter of doing away with the office of penitentiary in the Greek Church. The narrative which Hooker gives of the events in reference to this charge is evidently gathered from the pages of the historian Socrates. (See below, Socrates.)

Florence, Council of. (Chapter vi. § 9.)

This was held at Florence (after first meeting at Ferrara) between October 8, 1438, and July 6th, 1439. For a picturesque description of the Council, see Gibbon, *Decline and Fall*, vol. viii. pp. 98-104.

Gennadius. (Chapter iv. § 6.)

An ecclesiastical writer of the fifth century, and a priest of Marseilles. We know but little of him or his works, but he himself tells us that he had composed eight books against all heresies, six against Nestorius, three against Pelagius, treatises on the Millennium and on the Apocalypse, and a letter " De Fide."

Gregory, Bishop of Nyssa. (Chapter iv. § 6.)

Born at Cæsarea, in Cappadocia, about 331 A.D., and ordained by his brother, Basil the Great, in 372. He was appointed bishop of Nyssa, a small town in Cappadocia, and became a great opponent of the Arian heresy. In 375 the emperor Valens, who favoured the Arian party, banished him from his see; but he was restored by the emperor Gratian in 378. He was present at the Council of Constantinople in 381, and took an active part in its business, especially in urging the addition to the Nicene Creed of an Article touching the doctrine of the Holy Ghost. His works consist of treatises on controversial and practical theology, homilies orations, and letters.

Hassels. (Chapter iv. § 12.)

Hassels, or Hessels, was theological professor at Louvain. He was present at the Council of Trent, where he died in 1551. [C. and P.]

Leo. (Chapter iv. § 7.)

The reference is to Pope Leo I. He was born about 390 A.D., and died November 10, 461. In early life we find him sent to Africa with the letters whereby Pelagius and Cœlestius were condemned. At his suggestion Cassian (see above, Cassianus) wrote his treatise on the Incarnation against the Nestorians. The quotation made by Hooker from Leo's writings occurs in his

Epistles. He was chosen, as pope in 440, and used all his power for the aggrandisement of the Roman See. It has been well said of Pope Leo I. that "he sustained his dignity with so much splendour, vigilance, and authority, that he made himself more celebrated in the Church than any of his predecessors."

Maimonides. (Chapter iv. § 4.)

His proper name was Moseh ben Maimon. He was born at Cordova in 1135. He was a profound student of the Bible and Rabbinic lore. And it is pointed out by Dr. Jost, his biographer and critic, that what gained for him his widespread influence was his interpretation of the inner spirit and meaning of the Levitical law. His greatest work was a complete collection of Jewish law, entitled, *The Second Law*, arranged according to the Talmud in fourteen books, the first of which is prized by Jewish divines as of inestimable worth. They have a saying that "From Moses to Moses appeared no second Moses."

Nectarius. (Chapter iv. § 9.)

It is not necessary to add much to the account given of Nectarius by Hooker himself; but it may be stated that he was consecrated bishop of Constantinople A.D. 381. The account given by Hooker may be illustrated by a reference to Robertson's *Church History*, vol. i. p. 365. Nectarius died in the year 397, and was succeeded by the great St. Chrysostom. (See above, Chrysostom.)

Nicene Synod under Constantine. (Chapter v. § 8.)

This Council was held at Nicæa, in Bithynia, A.D. 325, and was attended by 318 bishops, and, in all, 2,048 ecclesiastics. (See Gibbon's *Decline and Fall*, vol. iii. p. 39.) At this Council was drawn up the Nicene Creed, with especial reference to the Arian heresies. (See Bishop Harold Browne on Article viii.)

Novatianists. (Chapter iv. § 8.)

Novatian, from whom the schism of the Novatianists took its name, was originally a presbyter of Rome. In or about 252 he was consecrated bishop, though irregularly, in opposition to Cornelius, the elected bishop of Rome. The view of the Novatianists was, as will be seen by a careful study of Hooker's argument, that "although lapsed penitents might be admitted to the Divine mercy, and therefore should be exhorted to repentance, yet the Church had no power to grant them absolution, and must for ever exclude them from communion; and that a Church which communicated with such offenders forfeited its Christian character and privileges." (Robertson's *Church History*, vol. i. p. 122.)

Occam. (Chapter vi. § 9.)

William de Occam, a renowned logician, and the famous theological reformer of the fourteenth century, was born at Occam or Ockham, a village in Surrey, about 1270. Little is known of his early years, but he is said to have been educated at Merton College, Oxford. After studying under Duns' Scotus at Paris, he became a Franciscan monk, and in this capacity was engaged in constant struggles with the papacy, maintaining the temporal authority of the French king, Philip the Fair. At length he was excommunicated by the Pope, and retired to Bavaria, where he died at Munich in or about 1347. He has been named the "Invincible Doctor" for his skill in logical discussion, and may be looked upon as one of the most conspicuous figures in the age in which he lived. He would, in these days, have been styled a Broad Churchman; and his writings, it has been well said, "illustrate the kind and amount of free opinion which maintained itself in an age of intellectual torpor and traditionalism." See also Mr. H. E. Malden's *History of Surrey*, p. 169.

Origen. (Chapter iv. § 7.)

Origen, one of the most eminent of the Fathers, was born at Alexandria, 185 A.D. From his youth upward he devoted himself to the study of the Scriptures, and when only eighteen years old, was appointed a teacher by the bishop. He soon devoted himself to critical labour on the sacred text, and after twenty-eight years' labour he put forth his *Hexapla*, or more properly *Octopla*, containing six different Greek versions of the Old Testament, the Hebrew text, and the Hebrew in Greek letters. He also wrote a *Defence of Christianity* against the heathen philosopher Celsus. He died in 254, leaving behind him the reputation of being the most learned of the Fathers. Owing to his departing in some points from the prevailing doctrines of the Church, he is the only one of the Greek Church Fathers whom the Church of Rome has refused to canonize.

Peter Lombard. (Chapter v. § 2; chapter vi. § 8.)

Born near Novara, in Lombardy, in the earlier part of the twelfth century, the actual date of his birth being unknown. In 1159 he became bishop of Paris, and died five years later in 1164. Little is known as to the events of his life; and his great reputation rests entirely upon the famous books of "Sentences," which were designed to be, and which gradually became, the manual of the schools. It will be noted that Hooker invariably designates Peter

Lombard as the "Master of Sentences." The books in question were four in number—dealing respectively with the doctrines of the Trinity ; of the Creation of all things ; of the Incarnation ; and of the Sacraments.

Sadeel. (Chapter iv. § 14.)

His real name was Antoine la Roche Chandieu, but, according to the custom of the times, he Hebraised his name to Sadeel, "The Song of God" (Chant de Dieu). He was born in 1534, at Chabot, a château in the Mâconnais. He soon became a convert to the reformed faith, which brought upon him persecution and imprisonment. Being liberated, he proceeded to Berne, and afterwards to Geneva, where he officiated as regular pastor. He next became court preacher and chaplain to Henry IV. of France, and accompanied him during the wars of the League. Upon Henry's reconciliation with Rome, he returned in 1589 to Geneva, where he continued to labour until his death in 1591.

Salvianus. (Chapter iv. § 6.)

One of the Fathers of the Church, who flourished in the fifth century. Neither the place nor the date of his birth is known. For some years he lived at Triers, where he married, but afterwards was settled at Marseilles. He was accustomed to write homilies for bishops who were not skilful in composition, which may account for the way in which Hooker ascribes to him the authorship of works commonly attributed to others.

Socrates and Sozomen. (Chapter iv. §§ 8, 11.)

Of these two, to whom Hooker refers as evidence in the matter of the Novatian controversy, the former is by far the best-known historian ; the works of the latter are published along with those of Socrates in the Paris edition of 1668. Socrates is a calm and impartial writer, and the seven books of his *Ecclesiastical History* are of high value, being the best record extant of the period between the closing years of Constantine, say 300 A.D., to the year 439, in the reign of the younger Theodosius. In the brief preface to his work Socrates tells us that he desires to take up the history at the point where it was left by Eusebius, and "to put the simple truth before his readers." Socrates speaks with fairness and candour of the Novatian party ; and being a trustworthy as well as a contemporaneous writer, he gives us a very good picture of what the Christianity of the fourth century really was. He was born about 379 A.D., and died in 458 or thereabouts.

Tertullian. (Chapters iv. §§ 4, 6, 7 ; v. § 1.)

Was the son of a pagan centurion of pro-consular rank at Carthage. He was born about 160 A.D. He was converted to Christianity and ordained presbyter in his native city. About 200 he embraced the tenets of the Montanists, and defended them with zeal and ability. His character was gloomy, severe, and fiery. He is described by Richard Hooker himself (chapter vi. § 6 of this book) as "a sponge steeped in wormwood and gall ; a man through too much severity merciless, and neither able to endure nor to be endured of any." His diction is vigorous, but the style is so concise that it is harsh and difficult. He had, however, uncommon power of intellect and emotion ; hence he succeeded in impressing upon Latin theology a type which it never lost. Amongst his works may be noted *De Pœnitentia*, which is the treatise chiefly referred to by Hooker, and *De Virginibus Velandis*, to which he also makes reference. The former was written before, and the latter after, his lapse into Montanism.

Thomas Aquinas. (Chapters iv. § 3 ; vi. § 9.)

Of French birth, his real name being D'Aquins. He has been called the "Angelic Doctor," and was the most eminent scholastic of his age. He was born about A.D. 1224, and was educated at the university of Naples. He became a Dominican monk at the age of seventeen, and after three years of study in Paris he proceeded to Cologne, where he remained until 1253, and was ordained priest. Returning to Paris, he began to lecture upon the Sentences of Peter Lombard, and soon attracted the attention of the learned, giving lectures in Rome and the principal cities of Italy with marked success. He was gifted with great mental powers, which he consecrated to the study of theology and the service of the Church. By far the greatest of his works is the *Summa Theologiæ*, which Dean Milman characterizes as the "authentic, authoritative, acknowledged code of Latin Christianity." He died at the Cistercian Abbey of Fossa Nuova, in the diocese of Terracina, 12th March, 1274, while on his way to attend the second Council of Lyons.

Trent, Council of. (Chapters iv. § 3 ; vi. § 12.)

This famous Council was held in the years 1545 to 1563, and promulgated what have been well called its "monstrous decrees," giving authority to Romish errors both in doctrine and practice. To counteract its influence, Archbishop Cranmer invited several of the most distinguished foreign divines in order to hold a sort of Protestant Council. Amongst these were Peter Martyr, Martin Bucer, and John A'Lasco. "Forasmuch as our adversaries are now holding their Councils at Trent," writes Cranmer to Bullinger, "I considered it necessary to recommend his Majesty (Edward VI.) to grant his assistance, that in England or elsewhere there might be convoked a synod of the most learned and excellent persons, in which provision might be made for the purity of ecclesiastical doctrine, and especially for an agreement upon the sacramentarian controversy."

CPSIA information can be obtained
at www.ICGtesting.com
Printed in the USA
BVHW041523171120
593515BV00012B/911